Police-
Community
Relations

LAW AND CRIMINAL JUSTICE SERIES

Series Editor: James A. Inciardi

Division of Criminal Justice, University of Delaware

The **Law and Criminal Justice Series** provides students in criminal justice, criminology, law, sociology, and related fields with a set of short textbooks on major topics and subareas of the field. The texts range from books that introduce the basic elements of criminal justice for lower-division undergraduates to more advanced topics of current interest for advanced undergraduates and beginning graduate students. Each text is concise, didactic, and produced in an inexpensive paperback as well as hardcover format. Each author addresses the major issues and areas of current concern in that topic area, reporting on and synthesizing major research done on the subject. Case examples, chapter summaries, and discussion questions are generally included in each volume to aid in classroom use. The modular format of the series provides attractive alternatives to large, expensive classroom textbooks and timely supplements to more traditional class materials.

Additional volumes currently in development.

Police-
Community
Relations

MARY JEANETTE HAGEMAN

Volume 6.
Law and Criminal Justice Series

 SAGE PUBLICATIONS Beverly Hills London New Delhi

For information address:

SAGE Publications, Inc.
275 South Beverly Drive
Beverly Hills, California 90212

SAGE Publications India Pvt. Ltd.
M-32 Market
Greater Kailash I
New Delhi 110 048 India

SAGE Publications Ltd
28 Banner Street
London EC1Y 8QE
England

Printed in the United States of America

Library of Congress Catalog Card No. 85-14631

International Standard Book Number 0-8039-2524-7
0-8039-2525-7 (pbk.)

FIRST PRINTING

1/17/86 *Beeker + Regly* 7.95

CONTENTS

PREFACE

Throughout many years of involvement with ethnic and minority groups, I have become increasingly aware that good community and public relations depend upon two elements: (1) a good program and (2) employees with a good attitude. In terms of both good programs and attitudes, this textbook represents the marriage between those who have done it and those who have researched how it was done and how effective it was. Gone are the O. W. Wilson days, when one person told us how to run a police department based on how it was done twenty years before. Authority cannot stem from one source; thus, this textbook will include citations from sociological, psychological, and criminal justice research. Obviously, many college courses, both undergraduate and graduate, have influenced me and have laid the groundwork for my understanding. Thus, there were many books, articles, interviews, workshops, and actual working experiences with different nationalities, both in the United States and in other countries, that have gone into my understanding of human behavior. It would be impossible to list or cite them all. Yet the materials directly quoted in this book should give the student some places to begin his or her own self-learning and discovery.

The lessons of the past have taught practitioners that good community public relations programs demand more than just the development of a program or the modification of one program to fit a specific locality; they also demand that individual agents in the criminal justice system develop and maintain a human relations approach to the job. For some, that may mean developing an attitude wherein the clientele has great worth. To be able to discipline oneself is the mark of a true professional. These are also the characteristics of a self-actualized person—a person who realizes the worth of a human life and does all he or she can to help that person grow and develop to the fullest potential or, at least, control others' behavior so that others who want to grow, can.

This text is designed around the idea that a community and public relations program is a drama of life. Relationships occur as if they were on a stage with (1) parameters, (2) perspectives, (3) people, and (4) partnerships. The *parameters* of that interaction are more than just the length and width of the stage. In this case, the parameters will be the setting for the stage or drama and the limitations (Chapter 1). The *perspectives* (Chapters 2 and 3) are the lighting, the spotlighting, and the focusing that will more clearly show what is going on in interactions. The chapters on *people* (Chapters 4 and 5) could be compared to the list of characters or the players. Finally, the chapters on *partnership* (6 and 7) will show how some of this can work together. At a time in our national history when incidents of cross-burnings, defacement or destruction of places of worship, and personal injuries and murders have been increasing nationwide, it stands to reason that all of us need help in knowing who is doing what to whom, and how public agencies can serve to create partnerships.

It is important to note that in this material, the term "publics" will be used. Although the term "general public" is more familiar, in reality there is not one public. Instead, our country is made up of different groups with differing attitudes, values, and expectations. Acknowledging this reality and using the term "publics," the student should be better able to deal with the realities of community-public relationships.

The purpose of this text is to combine many empirical studies with a depth of understanding of human behavior so that agents in the criminal justice system can develop working relationships/partnerships and maintain a positive attitude to protect their own health and well-being and to show goodwill to all persons. The most appropriate and permanent monument we can erect to the past victims of poor community and public relations efforts is the cultivation of a human conscience that will no longer tolerate tyranny over the minds and bodies of fellow human beings.

PART I

The Parameters: Community Relations— Concepts and History

1

POLICE HISTORY: ROLES AND PUBLICS' EXPECTATIONS

Frederick II, kings of Europe, and the Sheriff of Nottingham had no specialists in community relations. Instead, they had hangmen. In those early times, the state had to use force to make people do what they did not like to do.

The present state of relationships between agents in the criminal justice system and the publics they serve is based upon past relationships and present expectations of performance or roles. Were the early agents in the criminal justice system concerned with the publics they served? What kinds of communities, in those early days, needed what kinds of services? Today, what expectations of performance do communities hold? How do these expectations of achieving certain political goals differ with the constraints of the job and thereby affect community public relations?

The early English policing system, which was the forerunner of American society's policing system, established the heritage of local-community self-rule. The early kin policing system, which developed into the English tithing system through the Roman Empire, emphasized community-citizen responsibility. These cherished values set the stage for the modern interactions police have with their publics. The modern-day involvement of citizens in crime prevention programs is no happenstance. There are still citizens today who believe in an active involvement with their local police. In addition, the early American policing system did do work with publics in terms of both service and control functions. With time, however, the criminal justice system became more formalized, with departments of probation, parole, corrections, and the like, so that the police role included fewer service activities. This, of course, has contributed to the more recent dilemma or question of just how much police work should be devoted to encouraging citizen/community involvement and service activities. The section on the concept of community public relations, using managerial grid theory, should help to clarify what all agents in the criminal justice system can and/or might do.

In order to understand the present-day emphasis upon the use of public relations with community groups, the history of public relations will be discussed.

HISTORY OF PUBLIC RELATIONS

The historical roots of public relations can be traced to Julius Caesar's *Gallic Wars*. Those letters originally were written to explain Caesar's transalpine campaigns to a public that had no war correspondents, no institutionalized media. Thus, this informational operation was to help keep track of events (Hill and Knowlton Executives, 1975).

In the development of the United States, the *Federalist Papers*, along with many other newspapers, were used to help communication between the sparsely settled colonists for the purpose of independence. As the spirit for independence grew and the expression of that spirit was demonstrated in newsprint, the British authorities tried to control the press in the interest of the mother country. This was accomplished in two ways: (1) by licensing newspapers and (2) by censoring news, editorials, and advertising. Needless to say, conflicts arose and freedom of opinion and freedom of the press became important issues for the colonists. In 1734-1735, these issues were dramatized by the arrest and trial of John Peter Zenger, an American newspaper publisher, who was charged with libel because his newspaper had criticized British members of government.

> At his trial, he was defended by the famous Philadelphia lawyer, Andrew Hamilton, who argued that Zenger could not be guilty of libel if his statements were proven true. The trial resulted in Zenger's acquital [Bernays, 1952: 29-30].

Needless to say, the verdict had a great impact, for the Zenger story was told and retold.

Samuel Adams, the great press agent of the American Revolution, developed techniques of persuading the public that foreshadowed the U.S. Committee on Public Information of World War I. Not only newspapers but also pamphlets, posters, quilts, and flags were used. To build up public opinion in favor of independence, Adams used his newspaper and committees of correspondence, which he set up in eight other towns besides his own. It was through his paper, and through the use of the party machinery, that the Boston Massacre of 1770 and the Boston Tea Party of December 16, 1773, were publicized. Adams was a master at guiding popular resentment and grievances into the way of revolution. He turned popular prejudice into a united event of independence, so that his ultimate goal—the democratic state—could be realized (Bernays, 1952: 31).

DEFINITION OF PUBLIC RELATIONS

From the efforts of Adams, we can gain insight into the definition of public relations. "Public relations is the planned effort to influence opinion through socially responsible performance based on mutually satisfactory, two-way communication. Public relations is not sailing with the winds of public opinion, but rather navigating an institution through them" (Cutlip and Center, 1971: 11).

For Bernays (1952: 122), another eminent scholar and writer in public relations, the definition of public relations today involves three important aspects: (1) informing, (2) persuading, and (3) integrating people with people. Thus, public relations becomes an extended effort to integrate attitudes and actions of an institution with its publics, and of publics with the institution, for the purpose of goodwill.

Public relations in its narrowest definition is similar to publicity: informing the publics about one's organization. In its broadest definition, public relations means community participation. It is this definition that will be referred to when the phrase "community public relations" is used. That is to say, some of the publics in our communities have representatives who participate with law enforcement to work out solutions to community problems so that many persons benefit. In agencies in the criminal justice system, it may mean an interprofessional or teamwork approach to a wide number and variety of community problems (sexual assault, child abuse, and other domestic violence) in which there is a sense of common responsibility. For example, it may mean a group of medical physicians and emergency room nurses who, through a task force with police agencies, develop a kit for the retrieval of physical evidence from rape victims. Since police officers would not want to be trained as medical doctors to do pelvic examinations or autopsies, it becomes necessary for police agencies or agents to communicate their needs to another group of persons who maintain their personal and professional integrity and work with police to collect the evidence needed for police to participate in the prosecuting function.

The distinctions in the literature between and among the terms "public relations" and/or "propaganda" and/or "community public relations" is not always apparent. Some of the explanation for this derives from the history of public relations as a science.

Public relations came to be more accepted as a new profession after World War I. The developments in public opinion throughout World War I demonstrated that wars are fought with words and ideas as well as arms and bullets. Thus, public relations became equated with publicity men. People in business, private industry, and even government became conditioned to the fact that they needed "advertising," which became a synonym for publicity or public relations. Words alone were not enough to establish public relations, however. Words had to be backed by deeds. Hence, public relations evolved into advising the client on the "development of attitudes, directions, and even policies that he should follow in order to build goodwill with the public and to realize his social objectives more effectively" (Bernays, 1952: 82).

Later on, public relations experts emerged as those researching the emotions, character, and mental characteristics of the recipients of their message. Thus, one of the goals of good public relations persons was to be so sensitized to the "other" that the public relations persons could speak the other's language or, at least, address themselves to the other's needs or concerns.

THE NEED FOR THEORY AND PRACTICE

In police work, it is important to have knowledge about the entire theory and practice of community and public relations for several vital reasons. First, there is a direct correlation between citizens' willingness to report violations, to testify voluntarily as witnesses, and a police agency's operation, since citizen assistance is crucial to law enforcement agencies if the police are to resolve any appreciable proportion of the crimes that are committed.

Second, agencies in the public arena are in competition with other public agencies for money and other resources necessary for operation. Effectiveness studies done on specific programs do not seem to influence city or county commissioners who hold the purse strings, as do actual persons in the community who testify on and in behalf of the operations of the police.

Third, community and public relations enable individuals and groups to apply findings of the social sciences to achieve better understanding and integration of their publics. Too often, police feel that public attitudes are predominantly against them, when in reality, according to several studies, people are predominantly positive and supportive (Smith and Hawkins, 1973).

Fourth, public relations should help to reestablish the inherent pluralism of America. Groups do not have to feel the need to annihilate others in order to have "law and order."

Last, public relations should result in the reduction of conflict. Poor community relations can increase the danger of police work and assaults to one's person. According to the *1976 Summary on Law Enforcement Officers Killed*, compiled by the Federal Bureau of Investigation's Uniform Crime Reports, 110 of the 111 felonious killings of officers have been cleared. In a majority of the *assault* cases, *the assailant is known* to his or her victim. One would think that, due to the wide-ranging and largely circumstantial duties of officers, this factor of acquaintance between victim and assailant would have no bearing on death. The reality is that it does. In some regions of the country, the percentage of *the assailant being known to the slain officer* has fluctuated between a high of 50 percent and a low of 24 percent. As expressed in the *1976 Summary on Law Enforcement Officers Killed*:

> The familiarity between victim and assailant suggests what every law enforcement officer should clearly understand that his image and role in our society are distinct and unique. The impressions he leaves with persons arrested, detained, or interviewed in the course of his official duties are often telling, and could be the basis for some real or imagined grievance against him which later manifests itself, particularly in subsequent confrontations in an assault on his person. This is not to say that a law enforcement officer should conduct himself in a timid or patronizing manner. In the main, law enforcement duties are harsh and require, at a minimum, firmness and decisiveness, but these should at all times be tempered by a sensitive regard for the impact an officer's actions have on many persons with whom he comes in contact [Federal Bureau of Investigation, 1976: 2-3].

The anticipation of danger places a serious burden upon a law officer, one that may affect his or her physical and mental well-being. Working conditions that are dissatisfying can lead to high turnover rates, increased use of sick days, and a general decay of morale. No person likes having to work for people who verbally abuse him or silently send thoughts of dislike. Good community and public relations programs can reduce the stress of the job and prolong the lives of those who do the work.

In short, community public relations courses are necessary to help develop values, attitudes, and behaviors of appreciation for the worth of each individual person or group. No one group is responsible for good public relations, not even in police departments or agencies. Rather, as the philosopher Pogo said, "We have met the enemy—and he is us."

Having set forth a working definition of community public relations, attention can now be directed to our historical roots and the mandates they have placed on police in a democratic society.

POLICE HISTORY

When our Puritan forefathers came to these shores and helped to develop what is now called the United States of America, they brought with them certain ideals and standards. Some of those values included ideas about a fair and just society. England's Magna Carta was only one of the many important legal documents which their forefathers had developed to give individual citizens more rights and responsibilities and to reduce governmental abuse. The Constitution is thus no accident. Rather, it is a document emphasizing a balance of powers and citizen responsibility and involvement, an outgrowth of the prosecutions and persecutions of our forefathers.

COMMUNITY RESPONSIBILITY

The value we place in our heritage of local-community self-rule is the result of the historical development of several earlier policing systems that merged to become the early English policing system.

The earliest historical examples are kin policing groups, wherein small family tribes or clans maintained some type of social order. These early kin governments grew into civilizatons, and different civilizations rose to power and influenced others. Thus, Babylon influenced Persia, which in turn influenced Greece, which in turn influenced ancient Rome. In ancient Rome, social order was maintained primarily by the military legions of the ruler. As the Roman Empire grew and expanded, the corruption and social disorder in the military legions led to the residents of ancient Rome acting as law enforcement officers for geographic precincts by patrolling the streets in an orderly fashion. The duties of the individuals who maintained vigils were to keep the peace and to fight fires.

With the fall of the Roman Empire in A.D. 395, social life and order began to change. Throughout Europe, where the Roman Empire had been, warring nations emerged and invaded and plundered other areas. For instance, between A.D. 450 and A.D. 650 the Roman-Celtic people of the area known today as England were invaded by tribes from the continent known as Anglo-Saxons. During that time, the English tithing system was developed to maintain social order in that area.

The tithing system was a method of establishing the responsibility of each man for his neighbor and of the group for each man. This system of community responsibility through self-government was to ensure local justice and to protect the community from raiding tribes. Thus, free men were required to group themselves into a tithing, or group of ten families, for the purpose of maintaining the peace and sharing the duty of protecting the community.

To summarize to this point, tribalism gave way to feudal justice. The family was no longer involved in law and justice, and the state became the proper prosecutor in every case of crime. In England in Henry II's time, feudal justice was replaced by traveling justices, systems of royal courts, and royal writs. Custom had passed into law. The state as a political community possessed specific territories wherein certain laws applied—jurisdiction. The collective responsibility of the tribal law was replaced with the individual being held responsible for his or her behavior. Yet, even though the state emerged to apprehend, prosecute, and punish offenders, the community citizens held to their attitude of home rule—self-government and decentralized systems with civilians as agents in the criminal justice system. Although a national system of policing, *gens d'arme*, developed in France, our English forefathers rejected that national policing system through military units. The fear of national systems of justices, then as well as now, caused many people to be satisfied with an ineffective, decentralized, and costly organization. Today, the more than 40,000 policing agencies in the United States on the local, county, state, and federal levels are considered by some to be the price we pay for a community-oriented justice system and the freedoms, or checks and balances, we cherish.

SERVICE TO CLIENTELE

Besides the theme of community responsibility, a theme that runs through these historical documents is service. Many of the earlier forms of law enforcement included both *service* and *arrest and control* functions. Concern for the willing cooperation of the publics was exhibited in earlier police forces long before Sir Robert Peel immortalized that idea in his *Principles of Law Enforcement*. Even the early constables in this country had roles that included sealer of weights and measures, jailer, and announcer of marriages approved by civil authorities (Whitehouse, 1973).

Colonial America

For the most part, the laws of the American colonies developed within the tradition of English common law. The development of policing in the colonies was similar to that in rural England. In rural areas, county government was the political unit, and the sheriffs' departments were the chief law enforcement agents. Today, the Southern sheriff has lost some authority and/or police functions but continues to serve legal papers, collect taxes, administer jails, and transport prisoners. In the West and Southwest, the sheriff has retained political power. In practice, the sheriff may deal with rural—fringe and/or unincorporated—areas of the county. One of the most notable exceptions to this rule is the sheriff in Los Angeles County (Hart, 1980).

As the colonies grew and cities developed, night watches were developed. In 1636, a night watch was formed in Boston. Since it was not until 1790 that there were six cities with populations of more than 8,000, the policing units in the colonies were largely citizens—volunteers who worked the night to forewarn citizens of fire or other troubles.

Early Nineteenth Century

Because some of the volunteer night watchmen were lazy or indifferent, some of the major cities began to pay their night watchmen. In 1833, Philadelphia became the first city to pay both daytime and nighttime police. In 1848, that city reestablished the old, separate night watch. In 1854, the day and night watches were consolidated under one authority. Likewise, Boston, in 1850, consolidated day and night forces, as did New York City (1844), Chicago (1851), New Orleans and Cincinnati (1852), Baltimore and Newark (1857), and Providence (1864)—all pushing modern policing on its way in the United States (Souryal, 1977: 84-85).

In their histories of the police in the 1880s, Lane (1889) in Boston and Costello (1889) in New York both offer a number of examples that seem to have been typical of American municipal police agencies for that era. From their descriptions, one might conclude that the police were actively involved with the health and welfare of their publics. For example, Lane (1889: 17, 109) cited an 1824 Boston ordinance which provided for services that affected the health, security, and comfort of the city (for example, care of the common servers, care of the vaults, firefighting, door-testing, and the turning off of running water). In 1835, the Boston police took 506 drunken citizens home, handled 539 family disputes, gave shelter to 32 stray horses, and cared for 7 lost children (Costello, 1889: 294).

Early Twentieth Century

At the beginning of this century, a number of police departments continued to be the only agencies existing to help the publics in their communities. Departments continued to support charity funds, distribute coal to the poor, and assist wayward youth. The New York City Police Department initiated several community service activities which included establishing new city playgrounds, having private agencies open backyard playgrounds, talking to children in public schools, and, most important, assigning specific officers as "welfare officers" specifically to look after certain youth and correct their destitute home lives by enlisting the aid of some private welfare association (Fosdick, 1920: 369-371).

Since there were no state unemployment agencies or parole and probation departments, the police fulfilled those tasks as well. Prior to 1920, New York, St. Louis, and Los Angeles police departments maintained within their agencies parole and probation bureaus that were staffed by sworn officers (Fosdick, 1920: 377).

1930s-1960s

Between the 1930s and the 1960s, European immigration decreased and American blacks, generally from rural areas, began to migrate to the cities. As unskilled laborers, these persons were greatly needed in war production industries. During World War II, the nonwhite population of many urban, metropolitan areas doubled within a few years. The shifts in racial and ethnic population caused concern for police in many cities. Courses to train police in human relations, bearing such titles as "The Police and Minority Groups," were initiated by colleges such as the University of Chicago. In 1952, the Los Angeles County Conference on Community Relations reported on the specialized training in human relations or race relations in police departments in more than thirty major cities (Senn, 1952).

After World War II, some departments modified their police image. In fact, it was in 1950 that O. W. Wilson published his first edition of *Police*

Administration. Later, in circles of police reform, that book became known as the "bible of professionalism." The Wilson-inspired trend was to abolish foot beats and close station houses so that the radio dispatching of motorized patrols and command decision-making could be more centralized (Wilson and McLaren, 1977). Wilson's ideas were readily accepted by some of those trained in the military during World War II; the rule was to be a sentry manning the battlements in a "war on crime." The goals for departments holding that view of paramilitarist organization were clear-cut: apprehend the offender, bring the offender before the court, and assist in bringing the case to a satisfactory close. For some persons even today, this image is considered "real police work."

1960s-1970s

For many people who were born after the 1950s, it is difficult to comprehend what the situation was like in the early 1960s in terms of civil rights. In reality, it was an outgrowth of some situations in the 1940s and 1950s. For example, presidential executive orders were used to influence the areas of civil rights. President Roosevelt issued Executive Order 8802 so that defense-related industries would not choose employees on the basis of their race, creed, color, and/or national origin (Territo et al., 1977: 21). Needless to say, once an executive order takes hold, coverage becomes extended to other, similar areas (for example, federal contractors). During World War II and the Korean conflict, military units were integrated. People who were fighting for their freedom were not so quick to take backseats in the buses or to sit in the segregated parts of public eating places, as had been the custom. President John F. Kennedy, in 1961, again through an executive order, imposed the first requirement for affirmative action—a plan to implement and ensure nondiscriminatory employment practices and to correct past discriminatory employment practices (Territo et al., 1977: Executive Order 11246).

The reality was that there were many conditions in our society that added fuel to the fire for change. To illustrate only a few of the conditions and clamors for change, four areas of concern will be briefly discussed: the black civil rights movement, campus unrest, police scandals and the misuse of force, and the emergence of pressure groups for change.

The Black Civil Rights Movement

By consensus, the 1960s, with their violent confrontations and rioting in the streets, saw marked changes in our society. Young black males, according to the Kerner Commission (National Advisory Commission on Civil Disorders), had more negative attitudes toward the police than did white youth in general. Their unmet needs from the police paralleled similar failures by other public agencies (school, welfare, housing, and the like).

The black civil rights movement was intended to resolve the deeply rooted racial inequality in economic, political, and social conditions. Today, there is widespread agreement and documentation that the social disorders of those times were

> consistently triggered by the actions of police in dealing with blacks. Police response to racial disorder and other civil disturbances contributed more to these problems than to their solutions. In one sense, the protest movements and riots of the 1960s served to focus attention on the behavior of police and pointed increasingly to the need for more effective methods for dealing with inappropriate police actions [Cohen, 1980: 128].

Besides the widespread disenchantment with government in general and the police in particular, the black protest movement gave birth to many other ethnic and social pressure groups. The style and rhetoric of "black power" gave other groups acceptable models of ideology and action such that American Indians developed "red power," homosexual groups sang "gay power," and even a group of ex-mental patients developed a social group intent on "crazy power." Referred to today as the black civil rights movement, the crime and racial strife of that period brought yet other consequences—national concern, the passage by Congress of civil rights legislation, and the Omnibus Crime Control and Safe Streets Act of 1968.

In short, the black civil rights movement brought national concern to a group of persons often misused and abused by society and its agents in the criminal justice system. Unfortunately, many of those issues of the past still need attention and resolutions. Present-day research continues to find that the citizen complaints against the police are usually filed by nonwhite males between the ages of 16 and 45 (Wagner, 1980). Researchers continue to gather information concerning the need to determine why one group or any group of persons feels abused in the criminal justice system while the society in general, and the police in particular, are slow to transform that research into practical applications.

Campus Unrest

The youth movement was also radicalized during the mid-1960s, as an antiwar protest movement spread throughout the country, with its base on the already disquieted college campuses. "Generational extremism, embracing all the themes of peace, anti-authoritarianism and the new culture, peaked in 1968 and 1969, punctuated by the campus insurrections at Columbia and Harvard" (Daniels, 1979: 55). The campus ferment and antiwar protest continued, notably in the Chicago "police riot" at the 1968 Democratic Convention and the shooting of student protesters by National Guardsmen at Kent State University in 1970. Since 1970, the state has had to pay damages to persons who have sued on behalf of Kent State students. Thus, even though the tragedy brought an end to the youth revolution, it left a bitter taste in the mouths of many persons, both in and out of the criminal justice system, who continue to ask: "Is there no better way to handle these problems?"

Police Scandals and the Misuse of Force

Another condition of our society that has helped produce change has been the nationwide publicity given to scandals over police corruption and the violation of citizens' civil rights. Between 1960 and 1963, major cities such as Chicago, Boston, Denver, and New York experienced scandals over police corruption that received nationwide publicity, and then along came some of the worst race riots yet experienced—in Detroit and Newark in 1967, for example. In 1968, riots after the assassination of Dr. Martin Luther King, Jr., and during the Chicago Democratic Convention led people to believe that humanity and community relations skills had been sacrificed for professionalism. Numerous federal, state, and local commissions were demanding changes.

More recently, police conduct or misconduct in Houston, Philadelphia, and Miami, to name only a few cities, has brought national media coverage pointing to the continual need for proper selection procedures, training, and supervision (see "In Houston, Claims of Reform," 1979; "Feds Bring Brutality Suit in Philadephia," 1979).

During this period, scientific research continued to support the fact that deviance exists even in agencies in the criminal justice system, which are supposed to arrest other people who are not law-abiding (Barker, 1978). Some of that deviant behavior might have ranged from drinking to having sexual encounters while on duty to perjury in the courtroom to more violent acts of brutality against citizens (Barker, 1978). Some people argued that since only a few of these people—like bad apples— deviated from the established norms, the entire police force should not be held accountable (Atkins and Pogreben, 1976). Another argument advanced the fact that organizational deviance was institutionalized through the peer-group subculture and was therefore acceptable to some degree (Barker, 1977). Another explanation, as stated by the Guardian Civil League, was the inaction of others. Inaction might mean the lack of organizational channels to deal effectively with and investigate complaints, or it might mean the inability to reprimand or hold people accountable for their behavior (Culver, 1975). Concerned citizens argue that even though it is normal for some people not to be law-abiding, it is irrational to think that nothing should be done.

Pressure Groups for Change

Many groups have pressured the police and other agencies in the criminal justice system to change their attitudes, their role, and their image. Since many of the groups have represented legal, legitimate, "lawabiding" citizens, they were able to exert pressure. The federal government was one such pressure group (acting through the Law Enforcement Assistance Administration, for example).

The mass media have played a part in the clamor for change. Through the media's coverage of criminal justice activities, publics in the community have become more educated. In addition, legal decisions from the U.S. Supreme Court in the 1960s and 1970s have caused some agencies to change policies and procedures to maintain the national standards.

The problem of sexual assaults has caused agencies and citizens to interact and cooperate. The feminist movement brought the American people to an awareness that rape is not a sexual event but rather a violent act. Rape crisis centers were simultaneously organized by concerned citizens in many areas of the country. Those centers showed police, courts, and medical personnel, especially those in emergency rooms, that they had to interrelate and depend upon one another in order to prosecute rape. As more police and court agencies became aware of the victim's physical and mental well-being and their effects on his or her testimony, as well as his or her willingness to cooperate as a complainant, a more open system of intercooperation among many agencies concerned with sexual assault crimes emerged. As a result, attention was also drawn to national concerns such as incest, spouse battering, drug abuse, and organized crime.

In 1954, the National Conference of Christians and Jews (NCCJ) was instrumental in the establishment of the police-community relations unit in St. Louis, Missouri. This was the first such unit to be formally established in a U.S. police department. In recent years, NCCJ has expanded its involvement in criminal justice matters to include problems of courts and corrections. Today, numerous state and local public agencies for intergroup relations have also helped in this cause, including the National Association for the Advancement of Colored People (NAACP), the National Urban League, the American Jewish Committee, and the Anti-

Defamation League of B'nai B'rith. Many private agencies have also become interested in police-community relations and will, therefore, offer educational consultants.

In short, there have been many pressure groups both inside and outside police organizations. With this information, attention can now be directed to the present police role.

THE PRESENT POLICE ROLE

The present police role can be viewed from different standpoints, depending upon definitions. If "role" is defined as a set of obligations that accompanies a particular position or status in our society, then the definition of what a police officer ought to do will be based upon people's belief of what the position should do.

Most prescriptions and proscriptions for law officers are formally stated in detailed rules and regulations, general and special orders, and the laws of jurisdiction. Although the role of police is primarily a legal one in terms of crime, police agencies today, as they did in the past, perform a wide variety of community services. A common method of defining the multifaceted police role has been to identify the goals of a police agency. The National Advisory Commission on Criminal Justice Standards and Goals (1973: 104-105) has merged the traditional goals of the past with the element of policing in a democratic society to define the goals as

(1) maintenance of order
(2) enforcement of the law
(3) prevention of criminal activity
(4) detection of criminal activity
(5) apprehension of criminals
(6) participation in court proceedings
(7) protection of constitutional guarantees
(8) assistance to those who cannot care for themselves or who are in danger of physical harm
(9) control of traffic
(10) resolution of day-do-day conflicts among family, friends, and neighbors
(11) creation and maintenance of a feeling of security in the community
(12) promotion and preservation of civil order

A role is dependent upon the attitudes, values, and behaviors ascribed by a particular society. An example of the modification and definition of a police person's role comes from a newspaper account in Claremont, North Carolina. In 1963, the town's only policeman did not mind it too much when the town council required him to read water meters, check the town pumps, repair streets, and haul gravel. He called it quits, however, when they wanted him to haul garbage and cut the town's grass in addition to his other jobs. The newspaper account also noted he was paid $74.50 per week (California Peace Officer, 1963).

Some researchers have noted that the community's political culture can also define or structure the police role (Wilson, 1968). Other researchers have suggested that what police officers do is the result of how that person trained or socialized into the occupation (Skolnick, 1966; see also Niederhoffer, 1967). Still others maintain that an interaction occurs in which the police officer's role needs to be studied in terms of the demands of the immediate situation and not something inherent in the officer's personality (Bittner, 1967; Black and Reiss, 1967; Piliavin and Briar, 1964).

In order to answer the question concerning what kinds of expectations publics have, it is important to remember that for centuries, people have believed that home rule and democracy are important. It is not that the arresting of offenders or the custody of prisoners is not important. Rather, those activities should not occur at the expense of violating civil rights or the common standards of decency to human beings.

The fact that present-day police on patrol spend most of their time performing social work activities has been well documented in the literature. Yet it has brought to the forefront the argument and debate over what the police *ideally* should be doing with their time. For some, the "amateur social worker" aspects of the police role detract from the more traditional (proper) functions of crime fighting. When police work has been defined as "real police work," that has usually meant a high element of control. The resultant image of the police officer as guardian of our society has meant the search, chase, capture, and employment of violence under certain conditions. On the other hand, the police work that has been labeled in the literature as "unreal" or "social work" has often meant a lack of high control yet high concern for social services for people.

As long as the literature and the actual practice maintain this either-or proposition, police patrol officers are justified in feeling that they need only choose between the two styles and employ few, if any, community public relations techniques. In fact, a survey of police-community relations programs in 1972 showed that work units addressing police-community relations had been in operation between four and five years and did not function with a police-community relations advisory committee composed of citizens from the community. Although there were voluminous materials spanning diverse topics—such as operation of storefront centers, athletic leagues, counseling programs, preservice and in-service community relations training models, and police-minority group relations, to name only a few—Klyman (1974) was able to conclude from his research that, at best, most of these programs were really tokens when one considered the whole magnitude of what police-community relations could become.

Again, in 1979, police-community units were surveyed. Despite the cutbacks in the program, those police departments in the country with more than 300 full-time employees still maintained a community public relations unit. Yet a large proportion of the time was spent in school liaison and other liaison services and in research, planning, and public information services (Klyman and Kruckenberg, 1979). In reality, what has happened is that most departments have given many of the functions handled by the old police-community relations units to their crime prevention units.

A more helpful approach might be to apply managerial grid theory (Blake and Mouton, 1964; Hall et al., 1966; Tomaino, 1975) to police work. In applying this theory, five different styles of policing can be identified, and officers and communities can determine which style has the greatest probability of being effective in various situations.

The X axis in Figure 1.1 represents concern for control—security, search, chase, and apprehension at all costs. The Y axis represents concern for citizens—community and public relations. In this model, individual agents, as well as departments, might be identified as having a high involvement with citizens (1,9) or a high concern for control (9,1) or a high concern for both (9,9). Concern for control for police might mean arrest. This horizontal axis illustrates the concern for control, with ratings from low to high. A rating of 9 on the vector reflects a person or department concerned with only the image of "guardian of society," with large emphasis upon law enforcement tasks: search, chase, capture, and employment of violence under certain conditions. A (9,1) style would mean that a person is overly concerned with security or control.

The vertical axis illustrates a regard for citizens and social or public relations aspects. With a rating of 9 on this axis, the individual officer or department depicts maximum concern for publics and their special needs. The identified positions on this grid, such as (9,1) and (5,5), illustrate the variety of roles that exist between departments as well as within departments.

The (1,9) style (with its high concern for people) might be depicted by juvenile officers or school liaison police who try to resolve a juvenile's deviant behavior by effective referrals to other agencies. Indeed, society

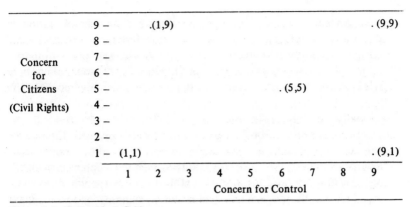

Figure 1:1 Police Work Grid

is willing to forgo concerns of control placed upon police if the youngster is viewed as harmless and in need of treatment or supervision.

Other agent roles might fall somewhere between the concern for control and concern for citizens. In the course of their duties, for example, some officers are drawn into situations that call for mediating human relations. The (9,9) style reflects an officer who, in settling a family dispute, fluctuates in the role to use mediation activities, referrals to other agencies, and control or coercive action, if need be, to protect himself or herself. The officer's ability to choose styles of behaving means that he or she is able to do a (9,9) style when and where necessary and a (9,1) (control or coercive action) if need be, to protect himself or herself and/or others. Instead of an officer always reacting in a (9,1) style, the model shows that other management styles of handling people—or the role—are available. Another example of a (9,9) style of policing might be the police-social work team used with abused children, domestic disturbances, the mentally ill, and other 24-hour crisis interventions. In that style of policing, with abusive children, the officer develops a proper case (gathers evidence) as he or she has been trained. Working with hospital emergency doctors, nurses, social workers, and other professional persons, such as child protective agents, the officer becomes part of a team effort to resolve and correct a particular community problem. In this style of policing, the objective is not to arrest parents but to reduce child abuse. If the parents are unwilling or unable to participate with the social agencies, then the decision to prosecute might proceed.

The (9,9) style is more than the community-police model of service (1,9). It is more like team policing, wherein the department itself is organized on a team model and the teams are integrated into the total community. Whereas the (9,1) style might create an "Officer Friendly program" to deal with a hostile community, the (9,9) style encourages the officers to think of themselves as members of the village community. The (5,5) style is less in concern for both control and citizens' rights than the (9,9) style.

Finally, this managerial grid theory could be used to determine placement in communities. Some smaller communities may, in fact, demand a (9,9) style followed by a (5,5), (1,9), and last (1,1). The "watchman," "legalistic," and "service" styles of policing referred to by Wilson (1968) could become operationlized through this theory and its testing devices.

The idea of this modern role grid is that the present-day role of agents in the criminal justice system mandates variety and flexibility. The argument should no longer be between those who demand "real police work" (as in concern for control) and those who have concern for people and their civil rights. Rather, the emphasis needs to be on when it is appropriate and beneficial to develop police-social work or other professional teams to handle communities' problems. Sniper or hostage situations usually do not call for community surveys. Rather, people in the community demand and will cooperate to achieve strict law enforcement, a (9,1) style. In other areas of interaction, however, people have different perceptions. A department, therefore, needs to be involved with the publics in the communities in order to define their role and gain support for that role.

The role grid suggests that all agents of the criminal justice system can improve different degrees of community public relations, depending upon the tasks they have to perform. It is not a win-lose situation; all can be winners.

SUMMARY

Public relations in its narrowest definition can be construed to be publicity—informing the public about one's organization. In the definition developed in this chapter, however, community public relations involves three important aspects: (1) informing, (2) persuading, and (3) integrating, people with people. Therefore, community public relations means involvement with communities and vice versa, such that goodwill ensues. From the expansion of public relations in other dimensions of our society, save law enforcement, came research identifying the emotions, character, and mental characteristics of a potential buyer. In applying this idea to agencies in the criminal justice system, agents have to be sensitized to the needs and concerns of the persons with whom they work and, perhaps, permit some of these individuals to be involved with the working of the agency (training, establishing policy, and so on).

The reason for taking this course, with its emphasis upon community and public relations, lies with the past. Our heritage from England has always included a deep concern for (1) local government and community participation and (2) service to publics. However, as our population shifted from rural to urban environments, so did the publics' concerns and needs. In the past, criminal justice system agents were uneducated and untrained to handle these differences in publics. Through the mass media and legal decisions such as those of civil rights legislation, people became sensitized to the unmet needs of blacks, college students, and persons who accused government in general, and police in particular, of misuse of force. Sometimes the nationwide documentation of such confrontations only increased the efforts of public and private organizations to provide teamwork to solve community problems. The present-day role of police was summarized by looking at the role through managerial grid theory—a high concern for control and a high concern for citizens and civil rights.

DISCUSSION QUESTIONS

(1) What is the relationship between real police work and concern for citizens?

(2) What could or should be done to resolve the problems created by the police having too many roles or roles that seemingly conflict with one another?

(3) What other factors in our society have been important for encouraging police departments to change to meet the clamor of citizen groups?

(4) All agents in the criminal justice system need to be concerned with community public relations. True? False? Why?

PART II
Perspectives

2

DISCRETION

What do the following persons have in common?

(a) The traffic officer is reading parking meters. The officer sees that the red flag in the meter is up, clearly stating that a law (however minor it may be) has been broken. The officer begins to write a ticket in the prenumbered ticket book. The officer knows that she is accountable to her supervisors and the court for each ticket; thus, she cannot simply tear up an already written ticket. As the officer writes the ticket, the violator comes out of the nearby store with small change in hand, claiming to be about to refill the meter. The officer decides to . . .

(b) The sheriff deputy in a jail is making his usual hourly bed check to make sure no one escapes from the facility. To be certain that there is a real person in the bed instead of stuffed blankets, the deputy has been told to look for "flesh." As the deputy goes from bed to bed, shining the flashlight in the faces of the occupants, one nonsleeping person directs an improper gesture at the deputy. A rule has been broken by using improper language or gestures. The deputy decides to . . .

QUESTION: What do both of these people have in common? ANSWER: Discretion.

Discretion is a by-product of professional judgment whereby individuals working in the criminal justice system are granted latitude in

AUTHOR'S NOTE: This chapter was originally written by Arthur J. Crowns, Ph.D., J.D., MSW. It has been edited and expanded by the author.

choosing among alternative possible actions (for example, to arrest or not to arrest, to prosecute or not to prosecute).

The purpose of this chapter is to provide a legal understanding of the necessity of discretion and how the drafters of the U.S. Constitution envisioned that need for delegation of authority. By looking at some of the factors that can influence a person's discretionary power, one can better understand how discretion, considered by some as a necessity, can also create problems, especially community relations problems.

LAWS AS AUTHORITY FOR ACTION

It is a cliché that our system of justice is one of laws, not men. In the final analysis, however, it is individuals dealing with individuals that makes the system function. Laws cannot enforce themselves; laws cannot punish, rehabilitate, or correct the offender. Laws provide only the authority for action, not the action itself.

The authority for action is based on the concept of "police power." Police power is the governmental power to make all laws necessary to preserve and protect the public peace, public safety, public health, and public morals (Thorpe v. Rutland, 1874).

The police power concept had its origin in the principle *salus populi suprema lex* (regard for the public welfare is the highest law). Every individual has a right to the free enjoyment and disposal of his or her property, but if an individual living in a populous community conducts himself or herself in such a manner as seriously to injure or destroy another, then that individual can be prohibited from so acting by government through the exercise of police power. Thus, in its practical application, police power proceeds upon the principle that each must use his own power so as not to injure another (*sic uters tuo ut alienum non loedas*).

In exercising police power, both state and federal governments are limited by certain important principles designed to prevent its abuse:

(1) State laws in exercise of this power must not violate any provision of the federal or state constitutions.
(2) State legislatures must not interfere with the exclusive jurisdiction conferred upon Congress over certain subjects.
(3) State and federal measures passed in the exercise of the power must not be unreasonable, discriminating arbitrarily against individuals or classes or invading private rights unnecessarily, but must be based upon one of the grounds for which the police power may be exercised, and also be reasonably adopted to that purpose.

A system of justice based on the concept of police power requires public officials who possess the ability to make responsible decisions. A simple society with total or near-total agreement on the laws to be enforced and how they should be enforced leaves little latitude for decision making by the public officials. However, as the society becomes more and more complex and more heterogeneous, as has our modern urban community, no consensus or agreement can be reached on many of the laws that control the individuals who compose the complex society. Thus, the need for public officials who can make responsible decisions as to when to use police power in dealing with the general public becomes extremely important. This decision-making power, when exercised, is usually referred to as "discretion."

HISTORY AND DEFINITIONS

The drafters of the U.S. Constitution, in their wisdom, were reluctant to grant any segment of our tripartite government too much "police power" responsibility. Those founding fathers were well aware of the tendency of government to become tyrannical. The Constitution separated government into three branches: the legislative branch, with the prime responsibility for making laws; the executive branch, with the responsibility for enforcing laws; and the judiciary branch, with the responsibility for deciding the issue of law. In addition, the Bill of Rights was to impose restrictions on government authority and police power (for example, the Fourth Amendment protects individuals from unreasonable government searches). In short, the founders of this country, who had for so long suffered unduly at the hands of other governments, wanted specific rights and protections for citizens who came under the influence and power of those directing the criminal justice system.

Police power was originally derived from the legislative branch of government, which made the laws that the public officials, in turn, enforced. As legislative power was originally conceived in the United States, the right to exercise discretionary judgment was assigned to the legislature alone. While courts in the nineteenth century held that Congress could not delegate any of its legislative powers to administrative agencies, it became apparent that this doctrine would have to comply with modern needs, and the U.S. Supreme Court, in 1931, held that "Congress cannot delegate any part of its legislative power except under the limitation of a prescribed standard" (United States v. Chicago, 1931). Thus, the Court gave birth to the "delegation of authority doctrine," permitting the legislative branch of both federal and state governments to pass down to administrative agencies under the executive the authority to exercise police power in enforcing administrative rules. However, what was overlooked until recently was how the public official, as an individual, would apply the rules.

When applied to police officers, "discretion" is defined as "the power or right conferred upon them by law of acting officially in certain circumstances, according to the dictates of their own judgment and conscience, uncontrolled by the judgment or conscience of others"(State v. Tindell, 1922). Roscoe Pound (1960: 925-926) defines "discretion" as "an authority conferred by law to act in certain conditions or situations in accordance with an official agency's own considered judgment and conscience—an idea of morals, belonging to the twilight zone between law and morals."

Discretion, simply stated, is the public officer's chance to make a choice between several options available in the exercise of police power. Thus, his or her duties compel him or her to exercise personal discretion many times every day. Crime does not look the same on the street as it does in a legislative chamber. How much noise or profanity makes conduct "disorderly" within the meaning of the law? When must a quarrel be treated as a criminal assault—at the first threat, the first shove, the first blow, after blood is drawn, or when a serious injury is inflicted? How suspicious must conduct be before there is "probable cause," so as to meet the constitutional basis for an arrest? Every police person, however complete or sketchy his or her education, is given the authority to interpret the law.

Finally, the manner in which a public officer works is influenced by practical matters: the legal strength of the available evidence, the willingness of victims to press charges and of witnesses to testify, the temper of the community, and the time and information at the officer's disposal (President's Commission on Law Enforcement and the Administration of Justice, 1967: 10).

LEGAL GROUNDS FOR DISCRETION

Making such distinctions is vital to effective law enforcement. Therefore, the law gives wide latitude to police and prosecutors in making arrests and in bringing charges. There is also the same latitude for judges in imposing penalties and for correctional authorities in determining how offenders will be treated in prison and when they will be released on parole. The law, in short, makes prosecutors, judges, and correctional authorities personally responsible for dealing individually with individual offenders, for prescribing rigorous treatment for dangerous ones, and for giving an opportunity to mend their ways to those who appear likely to do so. On the quality of the court and its officers depend both the individual's future and the safety of the community.

Most rules on the subject of discretion projected by administrative agencies and laws enacted by state legislatures require the public officer to enforce his or her responsibility on an absolute basis. The statutes of the various states which define the duties of law enforcement lack originality. Most of the statutes have existed for many years without the benefit of judicial interpretation. The most convincing evidence that the police person has been denied discretion to overlook infractions of the rules and laws is found in statutes that set forth the duties of various police agencies—sheriffs and city police are instructed to arrest "all" violators of criminal law. Other statutes read like this: that it is the officer's responsibility to arrest "all felons" or "all persons committing an offense in his presence."

Just as there are limited legislative guidelines on the use of discretion by police persons, there is also a scarcity of judicial guidelines in this important area. The courts have dealt quite frequently with the use of discretion by administrative agencies. Yet there are very few existing cases in which courts specifically focused on police discretion. The decisions affecting administrative agencies can be used as examples of the legal reasoning in this area, so that these rulings can be used by police officers as guidelines for understanding. These rulings seem to suggest several interpretations:

(1) The word "discretion," as used in statutory or administrative grant of power, means that the recipient must exercise his or her authority according to his or her own understanding and conscience (U.S. ex rel Accardi v. Shaugnessy, 1953).

(2) Discretion, as applied to public persons, means the power or the right to act in an official capacity in a manner that appears to be just and proper under the circumstances.

(3) Discretion is the act or the liberty of deciding according to the principles of justice and one's ideas of what is right and proper under the circumstances, without willfulness or favor and, as applied to public persons, means the power or right of acting officially, according to what appears just and proper under the circumstances (Tice v. State Industrial Accident Commission, 1948).

(4) A discretionary duty of a public person must be exercised with reason, as opposed to caprice or arbitrary action, since the term "discretion" imports exercise of judgment, wisdom, and skill, as contradistinguished

from unthinking folly, heady violence, and rash injustice (Commonwealth v. Brownmiller, 1940).

While the courts have recognized that the use of discretion by the police is proper, they have not set forth the guidelines that should control its use. Without guidelines, it is no wonder that some individuals, in their occupational performance, abuse the authorized discretion or create their own unauthorized discretion.

PARAMETERS AND PROBLEMS

There is no doubt that the exercise of discretion does exist within the administration of the justice system. It is practiced by public officials at all levels—from enforcement to corrections, from the federal government to the local government, from the police officer in a small rural community who permits a traffic violator to get off with a warning to a president of the United States who can grant a pardon to an allegedly errant past chief executive.

Even though police persons usually exercise their discretion, sometimes they do not. Officers do not always arrest people. Obviously, then, researchers are deeply concerned about predicting when or under what conditions an officer will exercise his or her discretion, or what causes a police officer to write up one type of offender but not another.

If the exercise of discretion could be viewed as a continuum, it would be difficult to find a person or group of persons who would typify the ends of the continuum: "absolutely never" and "absolutely always." Since most police persons operate somewhere between these two extremes, it is more appropriate and realistic to talk about parameters of discretion. "Parameters of discretion" is defined as the level of exercising discretion at which an officer is most comfortable. This level of comfortableness might also be called a "zone of tolerance." Each person and group of persons has personal zones of tolerance. It has been only recently, however, with the symbolic interaction perspective of sociology, that critical attention has been drawn to the tolerance limits of police officers. For example, in Piliavin and Briar's often footnoted research, the demeanor of the juvenile had an influence upon his or her subsequent arrest. If juveniles seemingly showed "disrespect" toward the police, the latter were more prone to use their discretionary power to arrest persons, as if to punish them (Piliavin and Briar, 1964: 206-214).

We all know that selective law enforcement is in part based on the subjects' attitudes and demeanor. Through locker-room stories, personal experiences, criminal justice experiences, and mass media, we could all probably note one or two reasons that selective enforcement—or the use of discretion—prevails. A number of authorities have also attempted to identify factors that influence the personal zone of tolerance for police persons (Schiller, 1972). The following are some of the reasons that police officers cite to rationalize their use of discretion or to explain why they feel pressure to view a situation in a particular light:

(1) Justice requires something other than strict enforcement of the law. The legislature intended the law not to be applied too literally but only to "wrong" kinds of situations or individuals.

(2) The law is absolute. It was enacted years ago and does not apply to present-day conditions.

(3) The law lacks community, judicial, and/or the prosecutor's support.

(4) As "God," the police officer can forgive. The highest authority has the powers to forgive, so why not his representative?

(5) The officer has the authority to bargain with the offender. In exchange for freedom, the state gets a good deal, such as a police informer or an excellent state witness against co-offenders.

(6) The police peer group has an influence on decision making. What work partners and friends think can influence the officer.

(7) The officer's supervisor can influence his or her decision. Most officers work under a supervisor, who in turn is responsible to a higher authority for progress toward the organization's goals and objectives. The supervisor usually makes progress reports on the employees he or she supervises, as well as recommendations for wage increases. Thus, the officer can justify his or her position by blaming the supervisor.

Other, less desirable, rationalizations for the use of discretion are the following:

(1) Due to the reward principle, some officers are corrupt. In exchange for money or a specific item of value, they will sell their public trust. This can also involve a person of influence. An officer can think that if he or she helps a person of influence, at some time in the future that influential person may be able to help him or her. This can also explain why some public officers overlook the behavior of women, seeing women not as persons but as sex objects. Thus, if they meet the right woman, they can be rewarded with sex.

(2) The officer might even be lazy. In this instance, he or she may think, "Why make work for myself when it can be avoided by looking in the other direction?"

(3) Some officers can be intimidated. They adopt the attitude, "Why should I get hurt?" or "No one cares anyway." This is especially true if the of-

fender can intimidate the police officer with blackmail or physical violence. Another factor that can intimidate the officer is the fear of having to be a defendant in a lawsuit. Many officers today overreact to civil rights legislation and will avoid a situation they believe might develop into a civil rights action.

(4) Some officers control their behavior because of a "loyalty factor." This is especially true when an offender is a member of the family or a friend. Thoughts of justification sound like this: "Blood is thicker than public responsibility," or "The offender would do the same for me if the situation were reversed." Loyalty may also be on a professional basis. Examples would be the police officer who will not arrest another police officer, or a judge who will not exert any energy to have an incompetent judge debenched. Loyalty may even be the result of ethnic group membership, resulting in overprotection of some groups while others seem to "get the book thrown at them."

(5) Due to the principle of empathy, some police persons use their discretionary power to be lenient and overlook a problem, or to overreact and exaggerate its degree of seriousness. The thought that usually runs through an officer's mind is either "There by the grace of God go I" or "Oh, my goodness, I did that as a kid, and that behavior has to be stopped."

(6) Another principle entering into the officer's handling of offenders is cynicism. That attitude may be expressed in terms of "Who gives a damn?" resulting in the officer letting the offender go or locking the person up with the idea of throwing away the key.

Needless to say, there are a number of problems associated with the police officer's exercise of discretion. Judgment is an element in all discretionary decisions; there is the possibility of error in any decision. Even though the decision is based on all known facts, most decisions are a calculated gamble. The review of a decision after the fact can easily be defined by others as "wrong" or "bad." The objection is usually in the form of the "but for" generalization—for example, "But for the decision of the public officer, the subsequent act would not have occurred." This argument proves that hindsight is better than foresight.

The police officer is criticized for not arresting a minor traffic violator who subsequently is involved in a serious accident. The prosecutor, the judge, and the jury are all subject to criticism if a defendant in a criminal case commits another crime after receiving leniency. The probation and parole systems are under constant attack because of alleged softness toward criminals. Under the Anglo-American system of individualized justice, offenders are treated differently depending upon their individual needs. In making decisions, the police officer must consider both the nature of the offense and the nature of the offender. We have a system of individualized justice, not a system of "equal justice."

Another of the problems that stems from discretion is that the individual officer, prosecutor, judge, or correctional officer may make a decision to evoke police power not from a real need but as a perceived need. In other words, his or her judgment might be based on the offender's appearance, attitude, assumed past relations, and stereotyped images, leading the officer to assume that the offender will be an assailant. Because of this element of perception, an entire chapter has been devoted to explaining this phenomenon. For now, it is important to realize that unless police officers are aware of their perceptions, they will have a tendency to make decisions that might amplify a racial or ethnic bias.

The area that has brought the most recent controversy has been the "fleeing felon" situation. The Supreme Court upheld the decision of the Sixth Circuit Court in Tennessee v. Garner (1985) by stating that state laws authorizing shooting of fleeing felony suspects are unconstitutional. The *amici curiae* briefs by the Police Foundation, joined by nine national associations of police and criminal justice professionals, the chiefs of police associations of two states, and thirty-one law enforcement chief executives, favored that conclusion. The briefs, supported by empirical research, argued that neither citizens nor law enforcement officers are protected by laws that permit the use of deadly force to apprehend unarmed, nonviolent fleeing felony suspects. The briefs also pointed out that without more restrictive shooting guidelines and review procedures, there is unnecessary loss of life, friction between the police and the communities they serve, and an undue burden upon police officers, who must make and live with the consequences of their discretion.

To prevent the continuation and escalation of the misuse and/or abuse of discretionary authority, controls need to be exercised. Department policy guidelines may be only part of the solution. If street patrol officers remain prone to assert authority when faced with outright hostility or the perceived threat of danger, then another part of the solution might lie in helping individual officers identify their preconceived notions and teaching coping styles with which they can reduce their own personal anxiety levels and maintain order and good public relations.

SUMMARY

This chapter began with examples to show that all persons holding occupations in the criminal justice system have some amount of discretion. By this is meant that the law provides an authority for action. The laws give public officials the right to make decisions as to when "police power" should be exercised. In 1931, the U.S. Supreme Court gave birth to the "delegation of authority" doctrine, permitting the legislative branch of both the federal and state governments to pass down to administrative agencies under the executive the authority to exercise police power in enforcing administrative rules. While our society was a relatively simple one, there was total or near-total agreement on the laws to be enforced and how they should be enforced. Today, however, as our society has become more complex, more urban, and more heterogeneous, the importance of police officers making responsible decisions as to when to use police power in dealing with the general public becomes paramount.

Even though police officers are given the power to make their own decisions, there are very few guidelines, either legislative or judicial. Because there are few guidelines, police agents are sometimes abusive in their authorized discretion. Thus, the concept of parameters of discretion was employed to describe the conditions under which most public persons can create a level of tolerance or comfortableness to justify the use of their discretion. Needless to say, this selective enforcement action causes problems, especially community public relations problems. Since justice is not blind, discretion can lead to a lack of uniformity, to corruption, and to the amplification of racial or ethnic bias. Solutions, therefore, stem from control by the department, through policy guidelines, and by individual police officers, who must better understand their own anxieties and needs and how these elements affect their perception and decision making.

DISCUSSION QUESTIONS

(1) Should police discretion be controlled? If so, how would it be done most effectively?

(2) What elements in interactions could be evaluated as discretion by some while others would call it abuse?

(3) A sixty-year-old black woman weighing 250 pounds, who has in the past been seen by a psychologist, has to be evicted from her apartment just before Thanksgiving. In her frustration, while talking with you, as a police officer, in her kitchen, she comes at you with a knife. Should you shoot her?

3

PERCEPTION, PREJUDICE, AND DISCRIMINATION

Is seeing believing? Can we trust our eyes to reproduce the external world accurately?

The answers to those questions will reveal that what we see and how we see are related to psychological and physiological variables. This chapter will show that perception is a complex phenomenon. It is more than simply seeing. Perception gives meaning to objects. It gives meaning to life experiences and the individuals or groups with whom we interact. In fact, as W. I. Thomas, an early American sociologist, pointed out, whatever people *believe* to be real will be real in its consequences. Thus, the concept of perception is extremely important to our understanding of community and public relations. Understanding the concept of perception helps one to understand how and why a person behaves as he does. Usually, the how and why of a person's behavior depends largely on how he perceives the world about him. The differences that arise between persons and among groups are often the result of the differences between perceptions (distorted as they may be) of life experiences.

Perception as prejudgment can become prejudice. Prejudice— especially negative prejudice—influences discrimination. To understand the interplay of these three dimensions—perception, prejudice, and discrimination—we will examine each concept in turn.

PERCEPTION

By definition, "perception" is a term upon which very few scholars and researchers agree. Allport (1955), for example, describes some thirteen different schools of thought among psychologists on the matter of perception. For our purpose, however, perception will be defined as *the process of giving meaning or organization to experience.*

To understand this concept better, let us discuss perception first in terms of a model and then in terms of a behavioral process. Under the topic of a model of perception, a number of interrelated variables will be discussed: differing sensory receptors, environments, stimuli, internal sets, and evoked sets. In the section dealing with behavioral responses, differences in people's perceptions will be explained in terms of communication, frame of reference, self-image, openness, defensiveness, and frustration.

A Model of Perception and Its Components

Perception is a complex, dynamic, interrelated composite of processes that involves the human nervous system (Robinson, 1972). Because biological and medical scientists do not fully understand the complexities of the workings of the spinal cord and the brain, we are limited in our understanding of perception. There are some things that are known. For a moment, consider the biological workings of the human eye. The human eye can handle the stimuli of nearly five million bits per second. This is done by the rods and cones of our eyes, which pick up signals from the outside world. These signals are then converted into electrical impulses in fibers to the optic nerve. Signals are sent, as though over telephone wires, to the visual section of the brain, the occipital cortex, located at the back of the head. Vision will, therefore, be damaged if that piece of the cortex, the nerve pathways, the optic nerve, or the retina is damaged.

One of the most important things to remember is that *the eye is an energy transducer*. The eye takes the energy of certain wavelengths of light (the colors of the rainbow from red through violet) and converts it into nerve impulses. It is not the eyes that see. Rather, it is the "perceiver" in the brain, commonly called the sensorium. While the eye can handle stimuli of nearly five million bits per second, the sensorium has limited abilities. The sensorium's resolving power is limited to approximately five hundred bits per second. In short, some stimuli are labeled by the person as important and others as not important. Some stimuli, needless to say, fall by the wayside. The perception is in the "eyes" of the beholder. It is not something naturally inherent in the stimulus object. Second, perception is an active process. An individual looks at an object from a particular stance or perspective until he or she is able to give the picture some meaningful pattern or name. Oddly enough, once the pattern has been established in a person's mind, it becomes relatively stable. No matter how long one stays away from the pattern, the moment one returns to the figure, the pattern is recognized. In short, an individual, consciously or unconsciously, notices certain stimuli in the environment, chooses to give meaning to some of those stimuli (usually based upon past experience), and uses those stimuli to produce a response or a specific behavior.

Perception is not the same thing as optical or visual illusion (Beeler and Branley, 1951). Some optical illusions are the result of the biological working of the eye. Thus, as one looks at the railroad track, for example, the parallel lines of the track seem to run closer together as they approach the horizon, and each railroad tie appears to get smaller. In reality, each railroad tie is nearly the same length as the others.

Perception, or seeing, is more than the actual gathering and recording of light. Seeing involves certain thought processes. These thought processes add complexity to the situation. Usually, what kind of sense one makes of a situation will have great bearing on how one responds to that situation.

Understanding the mechanisms of perception should help one to understand how witnesses to the same crime recall different versions of what happened and how one eyewitness's account differs so dramatically from that of another. Once a police agent can understand the selective perceptions of witnesses, then the agent may also be able to understand the differences in what he or she may perceive. The question then is: "How then do these differences arise?" The answer lies in understanding these five different, yet interrelated, variables: (1) sensory receptors, (2) environments, (3) stimuli, (4) internal states, and (5) evoked states.

Sensory Receptors

Differences in perception are the result of (1) fears and emotions, (2) the normality of the sense organs, and (3) sensitivity. If a person is not conscious or fully alert during a confrontation, then the information may not have reached the brain. If victims or witnesses are overcome by fear, for example, they may close their eyes. Needless to say, closing the eyes limits the reception of stimuli, and that, in turn, limits visual perception.

In addition, the quality and quantity of what is perceived are affected by other variables, such as fears and emotions, even when the sense organs are normal. How many more pronounced differences can one expect when impairments are present? For example, between 8 and 10 percent of the male population is color-blind to the colors green and red. Witnesses who report clothing or cars as gray may not be describing the actual color as much as the color they see through their color blindness. Many people may be color-blind and not be aware of it. In addition, some people's eyes are in better physical shape than others'. Researchers have been validating the fact that age affects perception (Coren and Girgus, 1978: 95). The explanation is that there are structural changes in the optical or neural system of the aging individual. These changes due to aging cause the eye to receive light differently.

Third, some people are trained to use one or more of their senses more acutely than the others. Perhaps the best illustration of this is the blind person who uses his or her hearing or touching senses more acutely. Likewise, some witnesses or victims have a greater sensitivity to sound, odor, light, touch, and so on, than do others. Some persons (for example, social caseworkers) have even been trained through their professions to be especially observant of people's behavior and speech patterns.

Environments

Different environments can also affect perception. The angle and the amount of light in a particular environment can affect a witness's perception. This important variable influenced the investigation of the shooting death of President John F. Kennedy in Dallas, Texas, in November 1963. Obviously, people's testimonies and films were dependent upon the location of the person and the film taker. Interestingly, to avoid this contamination in people's perception, scientists are now trying to reconstruct the shape and size of the late president's head. Through ballistics tests, scientists can watch bullets hit the reconstructed head and watch the movement of the skull from that impact. It is hoped that this information will be useful in determining how many offenders there actually were.

Stimuli

Even in a mutual environment, people see or focus on different stimuli. Some people may be more aware of colors, clothing, details, and the presence of people. Others might be more accurate in describing distances, physical characteristics, or the speed, make, and model of a car.

Internal States

Different people learn different things from past experiences. Our culture and subcultures, through the learning process, teach us different lessons about life.

Evoked Sets

Humans have a difficult time maintaining two thoughts or images that directly oppose each other. As in music, when two notes do not harmonize, these "notes" sound harsh to our ears. According to dissonance theory (Festinger, 1964), people will accept one idea and reject the other in order to establish a consistency to their psychic world. In other words, a selected distortion takes place in order to screen out features that are apt to disturb preconceived images. There are many examples of parents who are guilty of physical or emotional child abuse who still view themselves as loving their children. Often an investigating officer will be dumb-founded when he or she sees a child covered with strap marks. Finding it hard to believe that they were so unkind to their children, the parents distort the situation by saying something like this: "I was only disciplining the child." Fathers who are guilty of incest and who are otherwise law-abiding persons will develop strong rationalizations to handle this discrepancy and protect their self-image. One Catholic aggressor, when asked by the police why he had seduced his daughter instead of having an affair or hiring a prostitute, replied incredulously, "What? And cheat on my wife?" (Forward and Buck, 1978: 32).

Another example of this is when a police agent tries to issue a ticket for speeding to a so-called law-abiding citizen. If the agent harps on the driver of the stopped vehicle as being a law-abiding citizen doing wrong, it is harder for the driver to reconcile these two ideas. The chances are high that the driver will, through distortion, maintain that he or she is a law-abiding citizen and that the agent must, therefore, be in error. Less resistance will occur if the agent thanks the driver for stopping and does all that he or she can to talk about the behavior as opposed to the person and to place emphasis on the "here and now."

To summarize to this point, perception would be an easier concept to explain if only the process consisted of a straight stimulus "input" and a consequential "output." Alas, it is not so. A person's response or behavior is the result of the interaction of internal states with the environment. The individual, consciously or unconsciously, notices certain stimuli in the environment, and these stimuli support the values or goals upon which the individual chooses to focus. Since the eye can absorb more light cues than the brain can process, there are elements that go unnoticed. Most people "see through a glass darkly," as Saint Paul said. They do so for these reasons: (1) differing sensory receptors, (2) differing environments, (3) differing stimuli, (4) differing internal states, and (5) differing evoked sets. All of these variables affect witnesses', victims', and suspects' perceptions. Interestingly, these variables also affect the perceptions of those who work in the agencies of the criminal justice system. Thus, the perception of agents influences their behavior and those with whom they interact.

Perception in the Behavioral Process

Once meaning is given to stimuli in an interaction sequence of one's environment, then behavioral responses occur. Once one has had the senses stimulated, one formulates a series of symbols with which to express those experiences. "Experience cannot be transmitted as experience: it first must be translated into something else. It is this something else which is transmitted. When it is 'received' it is translated back into something that resembles experience" (Rapaport, 1950: 42).

As a general rule, the more objective we are, the more our perceptions mirror the perceptions of others. The more we use some objective measurement, the fewer differences there are and the more tolerant people can be of one another. For example, given a standard ruler of twelve inches, most people could measure the length of the pages of this book and come to some agreement on their size. In other areas of living, unfortunately, people are more subjective and lack specific tools of measurement. In areas such as art, music, religion, politics, and food, people are more prone to subjectivity. Lacking measurable, standardized scales or gauges or even standardized lessons, one often judges by one's own limited experience. In such areas, we find it hard to see something from another's point of view. In fact, we find it easier to threaten one another, or at least become insensitive to others, because we find it hard to "see it" from their point of view. Perception is not directly predictable from simple knowledge of the working of the eye. An understanding of some psychological variables, such as frame of reference, self-image, openness, defensiveness, and frustration, is necessary in order to understand what people see and how they continue to see only that which they want to see.

Frame of Reference

Carl Rogers (1951: 383-394) offers several propositions (paraphrased below) that serve as a rationale for the validity and utility of this construct: the frame of reference.

(1) *Every individual exists in a continually changing world of experience of which he or she is the center.*

For Rogers, each of us is at the core of his or her own world—the "everything happens to me" attitude. The human baby reflects this self-centered frame of reference. Some of the clients in the criminal justice system, even though they are physically adults, lack emotional maturity and thereby reflect this egocentrism. As public servants, we can never expect to be much more than our clients unless we grow beyond them. So long as we protect or shield ourselves from the reality that we, too, can be childish and want it "our" way, we will not expend energy in growing and will not have the energy to submit to the unknowns of life and the possible pain of change.

> (2) *The individual reacts to his or her world as he or she experiences and perceives it, and thus this perceptual world is, for the individual, "reality."*

Rogers placed quotes around *reality* to indicate that the perceptual world is not the "real" reality as much as it may be the way in which a person *believes* the world to be real.

> (3) *The individual has one basic tendency and striving, which is to actualize, maintain, and enhance himself or herself.*

For Rogers, the principle of self-actualization is the inherent tendency of the organism to develop all of its capacities in ways to serve, maintain, or enhance itself. This means that individuals try to meet their deficiency needs for basic necessities such as air, food, and clothing, as well as to develop toward controlling external forces instead of being controlled by them.

> (4) *Therefore, the best vantage point for understanding another's behavior is from that person's internal frame of reference.*

Knowing about a person's frame of reference can do a lot to predict or explain human behavior. For example, one particular officer knew this principle to be true and could therefore employ it in his task of going into a home to apprehend a person in order to transport that person to a mental hospital for evaluation. The officer found the person sitting in a chair "feeling the impulses and sounds of strange space creatures." The officer thought a minute, then manipulated the dials on his portable radio so that the machine transmitted "racket noise" instead of voices. Playing the radio over the head of the individual, the officer said, "This will drive away the creatures." After a few minutes, the officer removed and turned off the radio, and the individual meekly followed the officer to the patrol car to be transported to the mental hospital.

Knowing about frame of reference does not necessarily make it easy to utilize this concept. Perhaps the greatest single deterrent to one's accurately visualizing another's frame of reference is one's own self-image.

The Self-Image

One's self-image develops throughout life and is the picture one has of oneself. The self-image is often the response to the question "Who are you?" and serves as a contact with ourselves. When we think or talk about ourselves, we are usually referring to the abstractions we label as our "self."

In delivering death notifications to persons, many agents in the criminal justice system act disinterestedly in order to cover their own uncomfortable feelings of confusion and helplessness. Being the bearer of bad tidings, the officer usually takes a "drop the bomb and run" approach. When this is done, the agent who has delivered the news can never quite understand why the citizen is so angry with the messenger. After all, did not the officer do his or her duty? Nor can the officer understand why, after the person has recovered from the bereavement, he or she hates the officer.

Psychologist Morton Bard and others, working with major police departments across the United States, have developed programs to teach tactics for these death notice situations to enable the professional to maintain a self-image of competence. Such psychologists have enlightened police officers concerning the shock or stress to one's body when one loses someone very dear, pointing out that anger is a very common element of the grief process. They have taught officers to show compassion, to have the recipient of the message sit down, and to deliver the message in private, in a slow manner, and in an orderly fashion, so that each bit of information can be accepted by the recipient: "I am here because there was an accident—a bad accident, a serious accident. Some cars collided. Your husband was in his and was injured very badly." Presenting the situation in this way mitigates the impact and prepares the person for the announcement of the unexpected death. "We took him to the hospital right away. The paramedics worked on him. The emergency room personnel tried. I must tell you he didn't survive." These words help the recipient to understand that experts were involved and that suffering was minimal. "Even the direct statement, 'He didn't survive,' muffles without hiding the fact of death" (Weisman, 1979: 64-65).

Delivering death notifications in this manner does not take any more time and makes it easier on both the officer and the citizen. By giving structure and direction to the conversation, the officer conveys an image of order, control, and stability. With his or her ability to permit people their feelings as exhibited through tears, the officer shows strength through which other persons can gain support in a stressful situation. It takes a strong person, secure in his or her own self-image, developed either through natural means or through education and training, to be flexible—to be able to determine when it is appropriate to show concern for another individual through voice and body language.

Openness

Openness, like defensiveness, affects behavior. Openness means opening up—letting more stimuli into one's eyes, for example, to be processed into meaningful categories. Research using a simulated crime situation suggests that police officers who are more open not only remember more cues and clues but also make better officers, for they are more prone to be flexible instead of viewing people as "symbolic assailants." In general, the "officer rated above-average displays a flexible, low-anxiety response to stress. Rather than focusing on one coping style, reactions are geared to the situation, and range from 'vigilance' to avoidance" (Grencik and Snibbe, 1973: 35-39).

By opening up and absorbing, one permits the body to adapt to a stressful situation. In addition, more cues and clues about the other individual's behavior enter the nervous system so that one can more appropriately respond. It is important to understand that being rigid and uptight, with eyes focused narrowly, may cause harm to one's body as well as to community relations.

Defensiveness

Defensive behavior is the opposite of openness and can be the result of threat—real or imagined. Somehow, one feels that one or one's self-image is threatened. Although there are, indeed, actual life-threatening situations, there are also those situations that may not be actual threats yet are "perceived" as threats by particular agents in the criminal justice system. In nearly every police and sheriff's department across the country, there are some officers who seem to generate an abnormal number of citizen complaints in their daily contacts with the public. These complaints not only threaten an officer's career and self-image but also may become lawsuits against the department and the officer. In short, these complaints cause administrative problems as well as community relations problems, for they color the public image of all criminal justice officers, whether they be employed by police, court, or correctional agencies.

To understand more fully how an officer develops defensive behavior, Skolnick (1977) became a participant observer in a real police department, which he fictitiously named "Westville" Police Department. Through his work, he developed the concept of the "symbolic assailant." This concept was devised to explain a police officer's injudicious, authoritative reaction to languages and attire that the police officer has come to identify as threatening. Thus, the officer's defensive and authoritarian response was shown to be a defensive reaction to a *perceived danger* associated with the job (Skolnick, 1966). Much of the present literature dealing with the topic of police defensiveness indicates that age, race, demeanor, and attire are the cues by which the "symbolic assailant" is perceived. Cruse and Rubin (1972), in their major study of police officers in Miami, Florida, supported the idea that, for officers, one of the most "stressful citizens," or symbolic assailants, is a large teenager.

The importance of these studies is that some people, for whatever reasons, put up a "front" and act as though they are going to fight. Some officers perceive the front as real, even though it is not. Even more unfortunately, they act upon their own perceived fears. Many examples could be cited. Rodney Stark's *Police Riots, Collective Violence and Law Enforcement* (1972:15) should be consulted to see how police unlawfully attack persons whom they blame for a disturbing state of affairs.

Some research suggests that it is the young, inexperienced officer who is more prone to use controlling behavior (Cruse and Rubin, 1972) or more rigid behavior (Grencik and Snibbe, 1973). Thus, the young officer is more prone to involvement in assaultive behavior than is the older, more experienced officer.

A situation with a high degree of associated violent behavior and perceived threat is one in which two ore more persons are involved or there is a need to arrest someone in a group. Humiliation in front of friends or family may lead some individuals to strike out. Thus, getting the suspect alone may defuse a potentially violent situation. The attitude and the behavior of an officer, as exhibited in voice patterns (for example, calling someone by his or her name, in a calm manner), can do a lot to show the suspect that the officer does not consider this arrest a personal matter or harbor dislike for the individual. Rather, the officer is taking control over a situation that others are unable to control themselves. (For more information concerning how to resolve violent situations, see Russell and Beigel, 1976: 208-218.)

Frustration

No discussion of perception would be adequate without a consideration of frustration, "the state of the organism resulting when the satisfaction of motivated behavior is rendered difficult or impossible" (Munn, 1961: 710). Frustration is an important concept to understand, for when one is frustrated, subsequent behavior usually becomes aggressive. Some people have learned to handle frustration in socially accepted ways; others have not. Sources of frustration include other people, one's own self-concept, and one's physical limitations or personal defects.

Generally speaking, the more one has a large repertoire of alternative routes around frustrating obstacles, the less one will experience frustration. That is why there is such a strong demand for preservice and inservice training for those persons who desire to be agents in the criminal justice system. When individuals are shown alternative ways to handle situations that they have never before experienced, they develop more self-confidence and are less likely to feel that they have to prove themselves.

THE NATURE OF PREJUDICE

Where do people get their ideas of what black people (or any other group) are supposed to be like? What is prejudice? Is it normal to prejudge people or situations? If a person does prejudge individuals, how can that person be more in control so that those thoughts do not wrongly discriminate against other people?

Definition

Prejudice as a belief is the result of an attitude or feeling, favorable or unfavorable, toward a person or thing, prior to, or not based on, actual experience. Misconceptions are the result when one has assimilated incorrect information. Prejudgments become prejudice only if they are not reversible when exposed to new knowledge.

Normality of Prejudgment

According to Allport (1954: 9), prejudice is the direct result of this attitude (favor or disfavor) plus overgeneralization. Overgeneralization is a process of thinking with the aid of categories. Once formed, categories are the basis for normal prejudgment. Orderly living depends upon these accessible clusters of associated ideas, which, as a whole, have the property of guiding daily adjustments. Prejudgment is the normal tendency to form generalizations, concepts, and categories so as to simplify the world we perceive. Prejudgment is necessary for several reasons and therefore has the following characteristics (Allport, 1954: 20-23):

(1) *It forms large classes and clusters for guiding our daily adjustments.* We "type" a single event, labeling it within a familiar rubric and acting accordingly. Usually, this is done to enhance our sense of security by increasing the probability that *similar* situations are really *same* situations.

(2) *Categorization assimilates as much as it can into the cluster.* It takes less effort to overgeneralize. The mind tends to categorize environmental events in the "grossest" manner, compatible with the need for action. If an Anglo employer can generalize that "Mexicans are lazy" and use this as a guide for his daily behavior, then the Anglo employer is saved the effort of individualizing the workers and learning the real reasons for their conduct.

(3) *The category enables us quickly to identify a related object.* Every event carries with it stimuli that serve as a cue to bring the category of prejudgment into action. If we see a red-breasted bird in our backyard, most of us would think it is a robin. Given the cue "red-breasted bird," few people would respond, "Oh, that's the red-breasted duckbilled platypus from the West Indies." If we see a crazily swaying automobile, many of us may think "drunken driver" and act accordingly. If we see a person with dark skin, that dark-skin stimulus would activate whatever concept of black people that is dominant in our minds. If that dominant category is filled with negative attitudes and beliefs, we will avoid that person. Remember, the whole purpose of this process of categorization is to facilitate perception and conduct—to make our adjustment to life speedy, smooth, and consistent. This principle holds true even though we can all think of times when we made mistakes in taking cues and fitting events into wrong categories (for example, taking someone else's coat or hat when leaving a dinner party, putting the key of one's car into the lock of another person's car, or trying to smell a plastic flower).

(4) *The category saturates all that it contains with the same idealistic and emotional flavor.* The concept "tree" has, in addition to a "meaning," a characteristic "feeling" depending upon our experiences. This is why some people actually believe snakes are slimy when, in fact, they are not. This is also why some people have difficulty in dealing with homosexuals. The category "homosexual" includes, for some people, such characteristics as effeminate walking and talking, men wearing women's clothing and wigs, plus feelings of disgust, embarrassment, and disappointment, to the point where anger or hostility may be expressed.

(5) *Categories may be more or less rational.* An irrational category is one formed without adequate evidence. A child in grade school may form a category of Tibetan people as a result of a teacher or a textbook. The images may be erroneous, yet the child has done the best he can under the circumstances.

More interesting is the type of irrational prejudgment that disregards the evidence. Holding to a prejudgment when we know better is one of the strongest and most baffling features of prejudice. Some people, however, learn from the pain of bitter experience, and they strive to reference their mental field. They seek to be open-minded, so as to revise the categories that were erroneous and to avoid future pain, both for themselves and for other people.

There is, however, a normality of prejudice. That means that we as human beings, as a part of processing information, have a tendency to prejudge—to classify information into meaningful categories. Prejudgments are natural for human beings, whose eyes are able to receive more bits of stimuli than their brains are able to process. Thus, each one of us is carrying around "preconceived notions" of specific persons or groups of persons. Sometimes, one lacks firsthand knowledge, experience, or accurate information and will therefore permit assumptions, rumors, and fears to complete the image of a particular person or group. As previously mentioned, perception acts to draw the sensory data together into a holistic pattern. Thus, one continues to maintain the image through consistency. For example, in our society, some people hold to the idea that all blacks are on welfare. Some people are never exposed to working blacks. Even though surveys may discredit inaccurate information, some people hold to their previous ideas in protection of their self-image and in resistance to change. That is prejudice.

These prejudgments do not always involve minority groups, such as blacks and American Indians. Prejudgments can also center on the categories developed and labeled as "old people" "teenagers," "the handicapped," "gay people," and "women." In other words, each one of us has prejudices.

The hope is that, through the following discussion on theories of prejudice, the reader will become more aware of his or her own feelings and will feel more comfortable in exploring some of the categories he or she has created for himself or herself. Once one understands category making, with all its influences, one can better understand its effects on behavior.

Theories of Prejudice

There is no one theory that is complete and sovereign in explaining all human prejudice. Rather, there are ideas advanced by specific authors to call attention to particular important causal factors, without, of course, implying that no other factors are operating. Much of the sociological study of race and ethnic relations has been coupled with psychological analysis of prejudice and discrimination (Hraba, 1979; Simpson and Yinger, 1972).

In short, racial attitudes exist as much in the psychology of the individual as they do in the broader American society and culture. For this reason, several theories will be discussed: group norm theory, scapegoat theory, and the authoritarian personality.

Group Norm Theory

The group norm theory holds that all groups develop a way of living with characteristic codes, beliefs, standards, and so on. They also create their own "enemies," real or imagined, to suit their own adaptive needs. Thus, "we" suggests "in/love" while "they" suggests "out/hate."

The Puritan settlers of Massachusetts Bay, as early as 1630, richly documented the development of their society. The Puritans believed that their colony was a holy experiment that would serve to help others as they developed New England into the spiritual capital of Christendom. As religious and noble as these Puritan forefathers were, those community leaders responded to the so-called invasion of Quakers with a harshness quite out of proportion to the danger it actually posed. As with any confrontation situation, the reports are often hazy, yet documents show that Quakers were persecuted for nearly ten years. The first open indication of trouble did not occur until 1656, when two Quaker housewives were found in Boston Bay.

> The authorities had apparently been warned of their arrival, for the women were arrested, even before they had time to disembark from the ship. They were promptly taken to jail, where they were stripped of their clothing and searched for the marks of witchcraft; the next day the books they had brought with them were publicly burned in the market place. Not long afterward, they were joined in prison by a group of eight or nine other missionaries who had followed them into the Bay, and after a long detention (during which the windows of the jail were boarded to prevent contact with passersby), the entire group was thrown aboard out-going ships and hurried back to Barbados [Erikson, 1966: 115].

In short, the Puritan forefathers considered themselves the "we" and the Quakers the "they." They saw the Quakers as a "crime wave" and dealt with them out of the way they visualized the boundaries of their cultural universe. In this manner, then, the Puritans defined the Quakers as enemies and used the situation to create a more cohesive social organization which espoused specific beliefs and behaviors. Even today, some groups consider themselves the "we" and anyone else the "they." With this attitude, groups form resistance to other groups who, for example, may want to buy houses in their neighborhood. Claiming that the neighborhood will "go downhill," people will mobilize efforts to keep out not only ethnic groups but also such things as halfway houses for youthful offenders, runaways, and even handicapped children.

Scapegoat Theory

The so-called scapegoat theory stems from biblical times, when Moses led the children of Israel out of Egypt. During their wanderings and prior to the building of a temple in Solomon's day (about 970 B.C.), the priests of Israel performed the sacred ordinances on behalf of their people in a portable tent known as a tabernacle. Priests entered the outer chamber of the tabernacle every day, as required by priestly duty. Only the presiding priests who were of the tribe of Levi and were firstborn sons of a direct descendant of Aaron were permitted into the area of the tabernacle, called the Holy of Holies. Entrance into the Holy of Holies was on Yom Kippur, or the Day of Atonement. That day, then as well as now, was the most sacred of all days in the Jewish year. Its purpose was to offer up a special sacrifice within the Holy of Holies for the sins of the people. That ritual involved a series of events. The first was to prepare the high priest for his solemn duties. To accomplish that, he would make sacrifices for himself and his brother priests so as to make them symbolically worthy to perform their sacred functions. The presiding priests would then lay aside their priestly robes and don simple white tunics so as to return to the outer court of the tabernacle. In the outer court, the presiding priest would dedicate two pure and unblemished male goats—one to Jehovah and one to the evil one. Which goat went where was decided by chance—by the flip of a coin, for example. The goat dedicated to Jehovah was sacrificed in the outer court, and its blood was taken into the Holy of Holies and sprinkled on the mercy-seat and before the ark of the covenant. This, of course, symbolized the fact that Israel's sins were atoned for by the sacrifice (The Life and Teachings of Jesus and His Apostles, 1979: 390).

It is what the presiding high priest did to the second goat that is extremely important to our understanding of the scapegoat theory. The high priest went back to the second goat in the outer court and solemnly confessed upon it all of Israel's sins. The goat was then taken outside the camp and compelled to lose its way from the camp or else was literally destroyed by being thrown from a cliff. The transference of sins from the children of Israel to the goat has become our modern notion of a scapegoat. Today, a scapegoat is one who is literally punished for the mistakes or sins of another (The Life and Teachings of Jesus and His Apostles, 1979: Leviticus 16).

In modern times, then, the goat is replaced with human beings. The rhetoric heard is somewhat akin to blaming and projection. "I don't have any money. It's all those _____ fault." Allport (1954: 224) says that whenever "anxiety increases, accompanied by a loss of predictability in life, people tend to define their deteriorated situation in terms of scapegoats."

In analyzing scapegoating theories, Ehrlich cautions that frustration does not always lead to aggression. Why frustrated persons are unable to direct their hostility toward the actual source of blockage is not answered by these theories. Furthermore, when aggression is displaced, it does not necessarily implicate minorities of "safe" targets. In fact, nothing about the theory or frustration-aggression could lead one to predict what the target of aggression might be. According to Ehrlich (1973: 151), "prejudice and its concomitant behaviors are learned responses—learned and socially approved responses in specific social situations."

The Authoritarian Personality

The Authoritarian Personality (Adorno et al., 1950) is a classic study of the psychology of prejudice and discrimination. Since its publication in 1950, it has inspired a continuing scholarly debate. Part of that debate has included the idea that agents in the criminal justice system possess this personality trait *par excellence*. According to the authors, there is a prejudice personality, an *authoritarian personality*.

The understanding of a police officer who is motivated to intolerance, ethnocentricity, rigidity, and authority-dependence has had great practical, as well as theoretical, significance, especially in the area of civil rights. For example, if a citizen confronted a doctor or lawyer who was authoritarian, all the citizen would have to do is to discharge the services of that particular person and request another professional. However, when a citizen is confronted by an authoritarian police officer, the consequences can be quite severe. For some, it has meant their lives.

In the 1960s, one of the concepts associated with authoritarianism—in the investigation of police—was the "working personality." Skolnick's thesis (1966: 43) was that the "value conflicts of democratic society create conditions undermining the capacity of police to respond to the rule of law." Because of their exposure to danger, authority, the pressure to be efficient, and particular social situations, the theory goes, police officers develop a way of looking at the world distinctive to themselves—a "working personality." At that time, Skolnick did acknowledge that the occupational claims over one's daily existence extended well beyond official duties; he did not argue that it was a style of life, however. Today, stress literature suggests that the working personality can become a way of life affecting other spheres, such as an officer's home life (Hageman, 1978).

Niederhoffer, in his classic study *Behind the Shield* (1967), argued that authoritarianism is nonexistent at the beginning of an officer's career, but that it becomes a progressively stronger characteristic as job tenure increases. Niederhoffer suggested that authoritarianism is the result of socialization into the police subculture and the resultant personality of the job. It is as if to say: "We were not born this way. But you would become as cynical and prejudiced as we are if you had to work with some of the nuts we do."

In the thirty-five years since the publication of *The Authoritarian Personality*, the concept of authoritarianism has been applied to the criminal justice system—mainly to the cop on the beat. In researching published articles by criminal justicians, it was found that systematic and rigorous studies on police personnel and police organizations began in the late 1960s. In fact, with federal government mandates and monies and a general dissatisfaction with the police on the part of the American public, the decade of the 1970s became the decade of the cop. In the resultant research, published using scales to determine authoritarian or cynical personalities, three themes were identified: (1) organizational/individual debate, (2) theoretical connections and research into alienation and stress variables, and (3) research methodology.

The organization/individual debate theme that emerged referred to one side arguing that it was not the individual officers that needed changing or education but rather the entire organization or system. One of the reasons the organization/individual debate continued into the 1970s was that no research seemed to replicate another study. Because of some of the inconsistencies in the research, researchers in the 1980s have continued to look at problems in research methodology, particularly reliability and validity of scales. In addition, research has been extended to cross-national studies and into other occupational groups in the criminal justice system (such as prison guards).

There are more theories of prejudice than those already discussed. The richness in the literature is not purely academic. Much of the research has been conducted to understand how discrimination takes place.

DISCRIMINATION

The difference between the *attitude* reflected in the word "prejudice" and the *overt behavior* of prejudice, as in the word "discrimination," was summed up by an English judge in his comments to nine youths convicted of race rioting in the Notting Hill section of London:

Everyone, irrespective of the color of his skin, is entitled to walk through our streets in peace, with their heads held erect, and free from fear. . . . These courts will uphold (these rights). . . . Think what you like. . . . But once you translate your dark thoughts into savage acts, the law will punish you, and protect your victim [Rose, 1964: 79].

When there are love prejudices, little is said. When the hate prejudices develop as a counter to in-group loyalties, then the attitude becomes reflected in a behavior called discrimination—the differential treatment of individuals considered to belong to particular groups or social categories. First, attention will be given to the U.S. Supreme Court and how it has dealt with differential treatment. Then, derogation will be discussed, and finally, cost and social impacts.

The Role of the Supreme Court

Through the Equal Protection clause of the Fourteenth Amendment, many groups have gone before the Supreme Court to settle disputes. The clause implies that everyone has to be treated the same, even though some classification and differential treatments of those categories of people is proper.

Today, through the 1964 Civil Rights Act and the 1972 amendment to that act, no discrimination in education, housing, and employment can be made on the basis of race, religion, national origin, or sex (male or female) by agencies with fifteen or more employees. The Court is trying to do away with those past classifications that have developed through prejudice for "invidious purposes." It should be kept in mind that all racial, ethnic, and gender bases for classification are inherently suspect. The Court has ruled in several situations that the states, through their laws, are making irrebuttal presumptions, often to support their own argument of administrative convenience (Brown v. Board of Education, 1954; Cleveland Board of Education v. LaFleur, 1974; Washington v. Davis, 1976). That does not mean that the Supreme Court is abolishing all classifications. Some classifications are still legal. For example, under Title VII, sex cannot be used as a distinction unless it is a bonafide occupational qualification (BFQQ), such as a woman working in women's restrooms or physical fitness centers. As in the Griggs v. Duke Power Company (1971) decision, people are to be matched to jobs because of their ability to perform specific tasks related to that job; the decision to hire cannot be based on the employer's preconceived notion about black people in general, women in general, and so on.

Often, it is not until cases come before the Supreme Court that one becomes aware of how past classifications based on erroneous or no information continue to influence the way people treat one another. Studies done on the authoritarian personality report that prejudice and discrimination characterize the attitudes and behavior not only of the mentally disturbed but also of many normal people (Rose, 1964: 90-91). Perhaps that is why discrimination is such a difficult social problem.

Derogation

Many people may not intentionally discriminate against others. Yet through socialization, one develops a "language of prejudice" and thus uses derogatory terms to describe the members of another ethnic or social group. The old saying that "sticks and stones may break my bones, but names will never hurt me" is misleading. Articulated antagonisms serve to reinforce the images people hold of others. Furthermore, those sayings may have serious psychological consequences for those who are the targets of those words. Old-fashioned expressions that reflect this principle are numerous: "Jew him down," "He's Scotch, all right," "I've been gypped." Many persons are unaware of the way words continue stereotypes. The following riddle illustrates this power of words.

> A man and his young son are in an automobile accident. The father is killed outright and the son is critically injured. The boy is rushed to a hospital for emergency surgery. He is quickly prepared for the operation. The atmosphere is tense. The critically injured boy is wheeled into the operating room, where the surgeon on duty takes one look at the child and says, "I can't operate on this boy: He's my son!" What is the relationship of the surgeon to the injured boy?

Perhaps you have heard the answer, for the riddle is timeworn. Yet some people cannot believe that the surgeon is the boy's mother. Their disbelief does not stem from never having heard of a woman surgeon. Rather, their disbelief derives from the word "surgeon," which is emotionally colored in favor of surgeons being men—so emotionally colored, in fact, that the term "woman surgeon" is often used to distinguish between the two. Yet surgeons are not classified as "tall" or "short," "fat" or "thin." Likewise, surgeons are surgeons whether male or female. Truly, sticks and stones can break your bones and words can really hurt you.

Closely related are the caricatures of minority group life and exaggerations of speech mannerisms. Caricatures are not necessarily unfavorable. For example, some people consider Italians as great singers or good pizza cooks, while other people stereotype them as gangsters. The problem with any stereotype is that an individual and individual uniqueness are discounted, and the stereotype remains a stereotype to be used as a judgment against the person.

Humor—ethnic humor—is very much a part of our culture. In addition, television programs have given way to modern versions of stereotyping different groups.

Epithets or pejorative names such as "spic," "nigger," "kike," "greaser," "dike," "boy," and "ho" are extreme forms of derogation. These terms make up an important part of the glossary of hate instead of goodwill.

Cost: Social Impacts

Prejudice harms the victim's personal growth and the contributions that individual can make to society. As a society, we neglect to develop one of our most important resources—human beings. As a result of our failure to develop these resources, other countries taint our foreign relations policies by citing evidence that our society does not practice the democracy we preach.

Some of the consequences or costs follow:

(1) *Domestic hardship*. Domestic politics are hindered by racial and ethnic cleavages. Groups suffering from discrimination are often forced to live in slums, yet these people require a disproportionately high outlay of public monies for crime protection, health, and social services (Saenger, 1953: 22).

(2) *American dilemma*. People suffer guilt and frustration from the conflict between the ideas of our culture (such as freedom and opportunity) and the reality of limited opportunities for certain minorities (Myrdel, 1944: xlv).

(3) *Effect on majority personality*. Violence and hatred tend to brutalize those who practice these cruelties. The reality is that one cannot give pain to another without feeling some of the pain also. Thus, the violence and hatred done to other human beings tend to brutalize those who practice those cruelties. Humans tend to lose their sensitivity—they are past feelings, so to speak.

(4) *Problems of identification*. Minority children learn ethnic and racial attitudes at an incredibly early age and do not want to identify with a group that is considered "lazy or stupid" (Ehrlich, 1973: 124).

(5) *Cost*. The looting of stores, the burning of buildings, the destruction of equipment, the number of injuries to both police and civilians, as well as the number of deaths, all create an atmosphere of civil and social unrest that is detrimental to anyone's development or sense of well-being. Thus, the members of society pay costs that are hard to evaluate in dollars.

Solutions

Although this discussion has not exhausted the various explanations for discrimination, or for the cost we pay for prejudice, one thing appears certain: "Prejudice is learned" (Rose, 1964: 94). "It is to be found in the peculiar historical conditions and present political economic structures, out of which intergroup relations develop and are sustained" (Rose, 1964: 161).

Not all prejudice results in open violence toward minority groups; some discrimination is subtle. People simply avoid one another. Thus, achieving good relations between different persons, whether they belong to different ethnic, social, or sexual groups, continues to be a major problem of our time.

Allport views the development of mature and democratic personalities as a matter of building inner security (Allport, 1954: 441). When one's self-concept is free from perceived intolerable threats, or when these threats are adequately handled with inner strength, one can be at ease with all sorts of persons and can be more willing to trust his or her own perceptions. Once this has been accomplished within ourselves, we can reach out to change relations with others.

SUMMARY

Community and public relations demands people understanding people. For that to occur, one must understand human behavior, and that depends not on what is actually out there but on what the individual perceives as real. Perception is in the eyes of the beholder. It is not something inherent in the object that stimulates the seeing. While the human eye can handle the stimuli of nearly five million bits per second, the perceiver in the brain is limited to approximately five hundred bits per second. Thus, the process of stimuli selection is a natural reaction for the perceiver. Not all stimuli coming into the human eye are categorized as meaningful. Some stimuli fall by the wayside. Perception is, therefore, defined as the process of giving meaning and/or organization to objects, people, or whatever one experiences.

Since no two central nervous systems are actually alike and individuals are not connected to one another's spinal columns, differences in perception occur. What a person biologically sees is dependent upon the (1) sensory receptors, (2) environments, (3) stimuli, (4) internal states, and (5) evoked states.

Differences in perception are also a function of different individuals' frames of reference, self-images, openness, defensiveness, and frustration. A frame of reference is the particular way someone sees a situation. Understanding a person's frame of reference does not mean approving of his or her behavior. It means, rather, that by understanding how someone else views the situation, one can understand and explain his or her present behavior and, more important, may be able to predict their future behavior. Our self-image is how we think of ourselves and thus how we may feel challenged and resist change. One example is how police officers have to be trained to give death notifications so that their behavior portrays the image of order, control, and stability. Defensiveness, the result of real or imagined threats, has been discussed in terms of symbolic assailants. Openness, unlike defensiveness, is a process of allowing more stimuli into our eyes and thereby permitting more experiences to be processed. By opening up and absorbing those stimuli, an individual is better able to cope with stressful situations and gain more cues and clues about another individual's behavior. Usually, appropriate behavior can and does ensue.

In short, in understanding the process of perception, it is important to realize how differences can arise, to be natural, and to avoid having one's own self-image threatened. Thus, differences can be perceived, appreciated, and tolerated and celebrated.

In understanding the process of perception, one can better understand how these natural differences lead to prejudgment, or prejudice, and discrimination. Prejudice is a natural by-product of socialization. As one's nervous system differentiates stimuli, one learns—largely unconsciously—to attach meanings to those categories. Thus, prejudices are learned.

Since there is no one theory that is complete and sovereign in explaining all human behavior, several theories of prejudice have been discussed. The *group norm theory* was illustrated by the Puritans and Quakers in the 1650s: The Puritans created their enemies to fulfill their needs for survival and to hold their group together to develop a certain way of life. The *scapegoat theory* stemmed from sins or mistakes being transferred from the children of Israel to a goat and then the goat being killed. The dead goat figuratively atoned for the sins of those people. Today, as it has been shown, some people fail to use goats to alleviate themselves of their inability to forgive themselves; instead, they use other people and thereby compound hurt and pain in the world. The *authoritarian personality theory* suggests that there are some people who, because of the way they have been socialized, are extremely antidemocratic. People with this personality pattern are found in many occupations, including police work.

Whereas prejudice is an attitude—a predisposition toward behavior—discrimination is the behavior. In fact, discrimination usually refers to negative behavior. When prejudice becomes negative discrimination, wherein our society fails to develop the positive potential of all human beings, we, as a society, greatly suffer. Using the power of language, we derogate and stereotype others, which inhibits and discounts the development of unique individuals. Other costs include domestic problems and social and psychological problems for the persons discriminated against.

The solution begins with each one of us. When one's self-concept is free from perceived, intolerable threats, or when these threats are adequately handled with inner strength, one can be more willing to trust his or her own actual perception. Then, as one becomes more at peace with oneself, one can be at ease with all sorts of persons. Once this has been accomplished, one can reach out to send goodwill to others.

DISCUSSION QUESTIONS

(1) Prejudice (racism, sexism, ageism, and so on) can occur at the personal, interpersonal, institutional, or cultural level. Give examples.

(2) Can organizational structures perpetuate institutional or cultural "isms" even between well-intentioned individuals? How? In what ways?

(3) Can the ingestion of certain foods and drinks (such as doughnuts, alcohol, or coffee) cause distortion of perception? What implications do the biochemical approach and/or the stress literature have for police work? Do unstable police officers create problems for community and public relations?

(4) Pretend that you are now at the end of your life. Be aware of where you are, where you are going. As you begin to look over your life, the thought comes to you: "What have you done to promote racial and ethnic justice?" How would you answer?

PART III

The People

4

IMAGES AND
EXPECTATIONS

With a sensitivity to the mechanisms and distortions of perception, it is also important to know something about the people from whom one may want cooperation and/or participation. The purpose of this chapter is, first, to show some ways in which groups in a community can be identified. Second, there really is no general public, but rather several different publics that have different images of police and different expectations of services from the criminal justice system. The first part of the chapter will address sources of identification, while the latter part will deal with characteristics of publics.

SOURCES OF IDENTIFICATION OF PUBLICS

In order to determine who and what persons and groups are available in a community, several sources of identification are available: (1) newspapers and directories, (2) agencies, and (3) census tracts. Much information about a community can be gathered from these printed materials, which are free, public materials and readily available. Thus, money, time, and energy are saved, and privacy is maintained.

Newspapers and Directories

Usually, local libraries receive copies of not only local newspapers but also newspapers of other major cities. Sometimes, communities will have several different newspapers on a daily, weekly, or monthly basis, which can be used to identify specific persons or groups that might be helpful in supporting a particular program or identifying powerful, influential persons in a community who need to be contacted for their support. Newspapers usually tell the "good deeds" of persons who, when contacted by your agency, may be willing to donate time and/or money to help your program. The society page often reports which groups are studying specific social issues. Many of those persons, like the "child savers" of the 1890s who helped to establish the juvenile court movement, are willing to help in their own community.

Newspapers also tell which groups are displeased with the specific actions of others, when groups are meeting to discuss those issues, and what actions they are planning. Knowing their orientations makes it easier to address future issues or plan specific programs in a community.

Directories, like newspapers, are public information. Some directories list street addresses, residents' names, and their occupations. Other directories list social agencies, directors' names, the purposes of the agencies, funding restrictions, and services rendered. These directories are extremely helpful in referring clients as well as establishing "team operations" to handle specific community problems.

Agencies

Of the many agencies in a community that identify different publics and usually have a better idea of the attitudes and values of various persons, two need to be mentioned: (1) the junior chamber of commerce and (2) the United Way. The junior chamber of commerce (JCC) and even the chamber of commerce compile a lot of information to help prospective employers to settle their companies in a particular locality. Even though the JCC is known to publicize the positive side of a community, the organization can be most helpful. In addition, the United Way is a central social agency receiving community funds to help myriad public, social agencies (the Red Cross, the Boy Scouts of America, the Girl Scouts of America, Big Brothers, Big Sisters, and so on). This can tell you which groups are receiving money, how much, what their programs are, and what their restrictions are. United Way personnel can also tell you where the gaps are and which agencies could do more if specific funds were available.

Census Tract Data

One of the most vital comprehensive collections of information regarding our people is the U.S. Census. The framers of the Constitution, in Article 1, Section 2, established our nation's statistical system at the same time that they founded the government. The requirement of apportioning seats in the House of Representatives has been the basis for the gathering of information by the Census Bureau.

The process of information gathering, as well as the actual information, has greatly expanded since those early years. The first census, in 1790, taking twice as much time as was allowed, was completed in eighteen months by the seventeen U.S. marshals and their assistants. The delay was understandable, because the assistants had to supply their own paper, a substantial expense in those days, and search for the towns and villages when county boundaries were vague or unknown and roads and bridges were scarce.

Every ten years since that time, census data have been collected. Because of the history these materials provide, migration patterns and rural-to-urban shifts in population can be established, crime patterns can be identified, and racial compositions can be determined.

In other words, without leaving one's desk and driving through areas of town, one can learn a lot about the general characteristics of communities. From the census data, one can justify plans for programs and/or grants. In its "Case Study: The Location of a Playground," the Bureau of the Census showed how to present a plan to a city manager for locating a new playground in a neighborhood with a large number of children aged between five and fourteen who came from low-income families living where there was a lack of play areas (Teeuber, 1976). One might not be interested in playgrounds as a tactic for crime prevention. Yet the methods used for that example are the same ones others would employ for establishing storefront police operations, "get-down campouts," or any other community public relations program.

As mentioned previously, attitudes toward the police do not exist in isolation, but are a part of a much broader attitude complex. Those, in particular, who are most negative to the police often feel somewhat alienated from, and powerless in relationship to, the larger political system. People who are most involved in the operation of the system often feel more powerful in relationship to it and consequently less negative toward representatives of that system, such as the police. Thus, it would be most useful to identify, by whatever means, two or more interest groups who have some "convergence of interest" or "consensus of agreement" on goals that would result in program implementation. A five-step process could then be implemented, made up of: (1) identification of leaderships, (2) bringing leaderships together, (3) identification of areas of consensus and dissensus, (4) implementation of the program, and (5) evaluation of the program (Trojanowicz, 1972).

CHARACTERISTICS OF PUBLICS

Although the news media use the term "general public," that term is misleading. A more fruitful approach for practitioners is to realize that groups of persons can be understood by using several different variables. In the following discussion, variables of social class, population factors, and geographic areas will be discussed, so that generalities about desired police action and willingness to be civically involved can be noted.

Social Class

"Social class" is a nebulous term that is often operationalized by combining information based on education, occupation, father's occupation, and income. In a classic study of social class, it was found that there were upper and lower dimensions to each of the following three classes: (1) upper, (2) middle, and (3) lower. The hierarchy of Yankee City might not exactly fit that of other communities. Yet generalities can be asserted. For example, the upper class constitutes a small percentage of most communities. Most residents occupy upper- or lower-middle classes, or upper- or lower-lower classes. In addition, collective differences make one social class distinct from another.

Research has shown that as one's social class position rises, the following results occur:

(1) infant mortality rates decrease
(2) life expectancy increases
(3) the number of visits to a doctor increases
(4) the amount of yearly and lifetime income increases
(5) the desire to improve oneself remains constant
(6) the status of one's occupation increases
(7) the level of education increases
(8) facility in symbolic communication increases
(9) the age of first marriage increases
(10) the likelihood of voting in a presidential election increases
(11) the likelihood of belonging to a voluntary association increases (Warner and Lunt, 1941).

In order better to understand some of the more obvious social differences among groups of people as they relate to the criminal justice system, five basic classes will be discussed: (1) upper, (2) upper-middle, (3) lower-middle, (4) upper-lower, and (5) lower-lower.

Upper Class

The upper class typically enjoys considerable prestige. Respected individuals as directors of leading companies or chairpersons of boards are usually wealthy persons. Among the most elite upper-upper class, wealth is inherited and the idea of "old money" is used to distinguish these persons from those individuals who have recently acquired their wealth. With wealth and high prestige in occupational endeavors, members of the upper class usually live in the best part of town or create their own sections of town, so that they can enjoy a maximum of material comfort and privacy. Members of this class send their children to private schools and belong to exclusive clubs as a part of their family tradition. Their membership in such social clubs permits them to command resources that give them considerable leverage in determining community, state, and national affairs. Sometimes known as the "power elite," this group of persons has considerable power as well as financial and social status.

The elite seldom come into direct contact with the police, either as complainants or as offenders, except in the area of traffic violations. If and when the upper-class citizen does come into contact with the police, "high status offenders are the recipients of the respect and deference that citizens—including the police, prosecutor, judge, and jurors—have been conditioned to accord their equals or social superiors" (Hilts, 1971:20).

Even though members of the upper class are not often arrested, they do commit crimes. Some crimes are relatively nonviolent and stem from the upper-class citizen's occupation, such as falsification of reports, evasion of taxes, and the misuse of funds. Upper-class people have also been known to commit violent crimes, such as child abuse, spouse beating, and incest. The offenses of members of the upper class, "like the life style they lead, are of the type which involve extremely low visibility and involve victims who are unlikely to be aware of their victimization" (McDowell, 1975: 64).

Upper-Middle Class

The upper-middle class is made up of people who have climbed to their present status and occupation from lower beginnings. These active, ambitious people are extremely civic-minded and participate in community organizations. These community organizations often give their upper-middle class members a degree of local prestige. These individuals are very active in social interaction with peers in business and professional associations, as well as community groups. In short, these individuals have the attitudes of "activity, accomplishment, practical results . . . individualistic achievement with the framework of group cooperation and collective responsibility" (McDowell, 1965: 65n13).

Like the upper-class person, the upper-middle class person watches his or her behavior so as to avoid "embarrassment" or public ridicule. If he or she commits a serious violation, it is likely to take the form of what is popularly called "white-collar crime." When these individuals receive citations for traffic violations, they have a hard time accepting responsibility for their behavior, because it conflicts with their self-concept of "good, law-abiding citizen." Living in "good" residential neighborhoods with considerable material comfort, these people value privacy and often view the presence of a patrol car in their neighborhood as "unnecessary."

Lower-Middle Class

The lower-middle class includes white-collar clerical workers, small businesspersons, and salespersons. In recent years, due to the financial situation in our country, many families in this class have found it necessary for both parents to be employed in order to maintain their standard of living. Placing a premium on their self-sufficiency and respectability, combined with the fact that their energies are being utilized to sustain their position, these individuals are not very active in community groups. Most of their social interaction centers on family, fraternal organizations, or church activities.

In the past, according to research, a large proportion of police officers have come from this social class. Thus, there is a lot of support for police from this class; members of the lower-middle class generally view the police in a positive light and believe that the police are doing a "good job."

Upper-Lower Class

In terms of absolute numbers, this social class is the largest. It constitutes the bulk of the labor force, including both skilled and semiskilled workers. Although these individuals do make "good money," their occupations require relatively little skill, training, or education. Thus, these individuals, as a whole, have little influence within their community. They live in small houses, mobile homes, or multiple-family dwellings, in crowded neighborhoods that produce problems, such as family disputes, neighbor-vs-neighbors disputes, and the on-street parking of family cars and trucks.

These individuals are not typically social joiners. With their greatest concern "making it" in economic terms, they have little energy to work on community problems. Their motivation and present orientation cause them to overreact (for example, knifing someone in a bar brawl). Failing to sense the long-range significance of their behavior, and spurred on by a "subculture of violence," these persons take pride in their ability to resolve conflict by direct confrontation, as opposed to mediation or some other nonviolent conflict strategy. Needless to say, the police have considerable contact with individuals from this social class.

Lower-Lower Class

These individuals are often stygmatized as the "poor" or the "working poor." Not all persons in this social class are welfare recipients. These individuals become chronically unemployed persons because of their lack of skills, training, education, and, sometimes, health. Living in the most crowded, least safe, and unhealthiest conditions, these individuals are plagued with multiple problems. In one particular investigation situation, a police officer noticed that a family raised all of their meager furniture off the floor with bricks to avoid the rats. The occupants of the house erroneously thought that, because they paid the kind of rent that they did, they also had to live with the rats.

The individuals in this social class have constant contact with police and other social agencies. Most officers are able to predict future criminal or delinquent behavior on the part of some of these individuals (known as "accidents about to happen") due to the irregularity and instability of their family living patterns.

For some persons in this social class, it is poverty that characterizes them. Although the exact nature of poverty and crime and their relationship is complex, the reality is that crime and its by-products(such as victimization) are most commonly associated with the lower-lower class. The subculture of violence produces higher crime rates, and that justifies more active policing in lower-lower-class neighborhoods. The "high visibility" behavior of the lower-lower class often results in police intervention even when the police have not been called for specific service: "Many serious confrontations result because of the lower-working-class suspicion of the police, which often leads them [members of the lower-lower class] to resent police entry into affairs into which they have not been invited" (McDowell, 1975: 70).

Needless to say, the results of past interactions have developed into a folklore history and justification for present animosity between the police and the residents of these neighborhoods. Since many of these neighborhoods are composed of one specific racial or ethnic group, some persons naively assume that the problems center on racial or ethnic issues. The problem of the urban black population is not racism as much as it is a phenomenon called "class culture." This is not to deny that racism may well have precipitated the lower-lower-class culture, but rather to suggest that some of the solutions to the problem lie in understanding the class culture. Support for this class-culture concept comes from the Kerner Commission, which, while investigating the major riots of the 1960s, found that members of the lower-lower class expressed major grievances concerning: (1) certain police practices, (2) unemployment and under-employment, and (3) inadequate housing (National Advisory Commission on Civil Disorders, 1968).

To summarize to this point, different social classes have, generally speaking, different ways of viewing the world, and this, in turn, affects their behavior. Because police and social agencies have little contact with upper-class or upper-middle-class persons, the police often think the behavior of the lower-lower class, which is sometimes a panorama of human degradation at its worst, is the result of a specific racial or ethnic group. This may not always be the case.

Different regions of the country have different social class dimensions and characteristics. For example, cities large and small in the Middle and Far West usually do not possess an old-family (upper-upper) class such as those in New England. When a community in the more recently settled regions of the United States is sufficiently large, when it has grown slowly and at an average rate, then the chances are high that there will be some established old families.

All societies are organized in terms of social stratification. Our democratic society espouses the concept of class as if we all belong to the class of Common Man—the Great Middle Class. The founding fathers of our country were antiaristocratic, and that philosophy developed into a frontier philosophy in which a man could live on a piece of land, improve it for five years, and make it his. The Protestant ethic also helped people to believe that one could get somewhere through his or her own individual effort and hard work. The reality is that our society also includes some people who are in poverty, no matter how much others believe in the Great Middle Class.

The agent in the criminal justice system who has been taught that "cleanliness is next to godliness" often finds it hard to deal with poor people and their unclean living habits, or to even understand their plight. As poverty begets poverty, the rich get richer, and the poor get children, the agent often finds that experiencing poverty—seeing it, smelling it—is emotionally upsetting. As officers walk and ride beats in slum areas, they often develop a cynical attitude in order to cope emotionally with the mess that they see. Officers, caseworkers, and correctional personnel who make home visits soon learn to stand while taking reports, with the hope that the cockroaches (also known as "water bugs," "Croton bugs," "palmetto bugs," and half a dozen other "we don't really have cockroaches" names; Boraiko, 1981: 130) will not jump off the walls or furniture and land on them. The cockroach is, no doubt, in contention with the rat as the national pet of the poor. Designed for survival, these bugs will eat glue, paper, or soap when food is not available.

Good sanitation is probably the best cockroach control. Yet it is difficult to keep people and homes clean when food stamps do not provide for cleaning commodities—when what money there is, is needed for food for humans. Similarly, it is hard to expect cleanliness from families who have moved from rural areas into congested city areas, because what rural families did to keep clean or rid themselves of trash in the country is no longer appropriate in the city. Some people lack knowledge. Some people lack skill. And some people lack desire.

Poverty is and can be experienced by people in various social classes. Michael Harrington's book *The Other America*, for example, showed that wealthy persons from the upper classes could become alcoholic bums on skid row and that college graduate students from various social classes could and would sometimes have to endure poverty while they earned their degree (Harrington, 1969).

Today, many woman-headed families also do not fare too well economically. A woman-headed family may be the result of divorce, widowhood, or separation. Even though her family may have been from the great middle class, the employability of the female may place her and her children in areas of the city that are considered poor.

People who live in rural areas also suffer from an economic condition that has psychological and social consequences. Tourists using the main highways and superhighways never see the pitiful surroundings of poverty. They never realize that the people there are often undereducated, underprivileged, lacking medical care, and in the process of being forced from the land to jobs in the city, where they will become social misfits (Harrington, 1969). The important point of this discussion is that, regardless of people's previous social class, certain groups of people at certain times in their lives experience poverty and will come into the process of the criminal justice system. Groups of persons with limited economic resources, skid-row alcoholics, minorities, rural people such as those in Appalachia, the aged, students, single women heads of household, and unemployable, older males usually are politically invisible. They are usually cynical and exploited. As Sargent Shriver (1965) aptly stated:

> Poverty is not just a matter of income, or need, or lack of opportunity. It is also a relationship to society, the inability to cope with hostile or indifferent institutions. It is lack of dignity and vulnerability to injustice.

The great War on Poverty in the 1960s was never won; poverty continues in our society.

Many excellent books have been written on poverty. Most sociology courses in social problems deal with America's poor and the cycle of poverty, which includes poor housing, poor health, poor education, and poor jobs. It is not the point of this section to discuss all of that material. Rather, the concept of poverty has been discussed so that people can understand that other people in our society might be different and might also be motivated by a different lifestyle because of their economic resources. People outside the lower class who experience poverty usually do so as the result of some external circumstances (involuntary unemployment, prolonged illness, death or divorce of a breadwinner, or some other misfortune; Banfield, 1970: 126). In addition, poverty is highly associated with many ethnic and minority groups, and therefore demands our understanding.

Population Factors

In the following discussion of citizens and the services they demand, other characteristics of population will be discussed: population density, age and sex distribution, and shifts in population.

Population Density

Population density is the number of persons per square mile of land use. Knowing how many people live in an area—the size of the city—often produces distortions about that population. When one knows more about the land use and how many people are using that land, more accurate predictions can be made about those areas. For example, population density will affect population increase and expansion. Greater population density associated with lower income, lower socioeconomic status, and higher rates of unemployment and underemployment means greater demands for police services. Higher crime rates have consistently been associated with densely populated inner-urban areas, regardless of the ethnic or racial characteristics of the residents. A geographer who has studied crime and population density points to the inadequacy of the conventional measure of population density. In its place, he recommends a measurement—a crowding index—of persons per room, because "it approximates human reactions to space and is more likely to help us predict areas of social pathology" (Harries, 1974: 83).

Age and Sex Structure

The most successful variable for predicting criminal behavior is sex, or gender. Males consistently act more violently than females. That does not mean that females cannot be wild and wicked. It simply means that, at present, statistics show that there are more males arrested and processed through the system for most crimes in comparison to females.

The second most important statistical variable is age. As age increases, the crime rate decreases for all offenses except sex crimes.

This information, in combination with information about the location of young males in a city, can tell one where to establish crime prevention programs. When one adds information about young males who also live in crowded living conditions, in an environment of lower levels of education, diminished opportunities, and lower socioeconomic class, then one can also predict higher arrest rates and higher rates of official delinquency.

The age and sex structures of a population do not remain constant. They change. Congress's Joint Economic Committee has investigated population shifts in terms of age for the U.S. population. Assuming that there is no large immigration of relatively young populations, the Committee states:

> The median age of the United States population—30 in 1979—will be 33 in 1990 and will rise to 36 in 2000. Whereas attention in the two prior decades centered on the young people, in the 1980's much of it will return to the 35-45 age group and in the 1990's will likely focus on the 45-55 age group [Institute for Socioeconomic Studies, 1981: 4].

The shift from "baby boomers" to more "gray hairs" should ease unemployment among teenagers and young adults. It should also reduce the past strain in the public school system, but at the same time it will cause universities to look for students from other population groups in order to maintain a student clientele. The phenomenon of more older persons will not be evenly distributed. Whites will have more older persons and fewer younger persons, but other minorities will have a more youthful population.

Many senior citizens lead vigorous lives and thereby pass unnoticed by agents in the criminal justice system. If an older person does come to the attention of a police officer, it is often the very old who are also very poor and sick. This, then, leaves an impression with police officers that all persons who are elderly are characterized by senility and sickness. More pointedly, senility—a word once used to describe the older person whose mental capacity was diminished—is fading into disuse. Many signs and symptoms formerly ascribed to a state of "old age" are now being more accurately diagnosed and treated. Senility is not inevitable for people who get older. Similarly, the crippling disease of arthritis can also be experienced by children and babies; our society is beginning to see arthritis as a condition needing research and a cure. Heretofore, many persons in society erroneously accepted sickness as a condition of old age. It is true that, as humans age, there is a tendency to develop infirmities and a diminishment of physical capabilities. Yet many senior citizens learn to cope with minor infirmities and continue to live full, meaningful lives.

Among groups representing senior citizens and their interests has been the Gray Panthers. Their national leader, Margaret Kum (aged seventy-seven in 1983), is an excellent example of a politically active, concerned senior citizen. Likewise, the American Association of Retired Persons (ARP) and the National Council of Senior Citizens are concerned with issues facing older people. The 1983 discussion of changes in the social security system brought together many national groups as well as other senior citizens' organizations, labor unions, and church groups.

The increased attention to older Americans has been accompanied by more research and more programs. Studies done on rates of victimization have showed that the elderly are less likely than younger persons to be victims of crimes against the person. On the other hand, numerous studies indicate higher victimization rates in particular crime categories for senior citizens living in the inner city. Categories include strong-arm robbery, purse snatching, vandalism, and assault; in addition, senior citizens are prone to be victims of con games, thefts, burglaries, harassment, and extortion (Young Rifai, 1976). In Philadelphia, a decoy program called the "grandpop patrol" has been developed wherein volunteer police officers disguise themselves as elderly citizens. Before going to a selected area, the "grandpop" is wired with communications equipment. This permits him to communicate with a backup team of detectives. Needless to say, the grandpop squad acts to reduce attacks on older people (Fox et al., 1978).

An area of victimization that has recently been investigated and will, in the future, be a topic of great concern is the abuse of elderly persons. In 1981, the U.S. House Select Committee on Aging conducted an examination of this hidden problem, in which abused elderly persons were reluctant to admit that their children, their loved ones, and those entrusted with their care had assaulted them. Examples of abuse are theft of social security checks, assault, fraud, larceny, rape, and murder. In those cases reported, the victims were likely to be seventy-five years or older and to live in a position of dependency upon others for care and protection. The abuser, in addition, was under stress such as alcoholism, drug addiction, marital problems, or long-term financial difficulties. Moreover, the committee found that

> the majority of . . . the states' statutes relating to adult protective services are ineffective and that the needs of the abused elderly are not being met. The overwhelming majority of state studies recommended legislation to establish model mandatory reporting requirements for abuse of elderly persons. . . . The United States Congress should enact H.R. 769, the Prevention, Identification, and Treatment of Elder Abuse Act of 1981. The bill provides for the financial assistance for programs of prevention, identification, and treatment, and would provide for the establishment of a National Center for Elder Abuse with the task of developing a model statute [U.S. House Select Committee on Aging, 1981].

Regardless of the statistical fact of legal victimization, older persons have a high fear of crime (Clemente and Kleiman, 1978). The fear among older Americans is the product of external and internal realities faced by these people (Jaycox, 1978). Since older Americans have declining functional competencies and declining financial resources, a victim of purse snatching, for example, may be without finances for an entire month. Injuries inflicted by an assailant on an older victim can cause lasting and permanent disability. Thus, becoming a victim leaves devastating results. These realities cause many older persons living alone in deteriorating urban environments to become prisoners in their own homes or apartments, because they fear to venture out of their dwellings (Harel and Broderick, 1980).

Strong community support networks and family contact can significantly reduce the level of fear and the impact of victimization. This emotional and physical support is extremely important for older Americans. In addition, older citizens lack knowledge about the functions of the criminal justice system. Older citizens are, therefore, supportive of the criminal justice system in theory, but tend to avoid contact in practice (Young Rifai, 1976).

Criminal justice agencies throughout the United States have developed programs for the elderly to deal with their fear of crime and their victimization. In New York City, the police department has crime prevention programs, postincident victim assistance, special police department investigation and arrest programs, victim and witness assistance projects, court actions to limit appearance, and court monitoring (Nova Institute, 1978).

The Waterford (New York) Police Department has also established a senior citizen crime prevention program. This program consists of lectures and films. In addition, presentations are offered to persons confined in the home (Fox et al., 1978).

The Cuyahoga County Commissioners Senior Safety and Security Programs (SSSP) trains senior citizens in crime prevention techniques and behavior (Harel and Broderick, 1980: 35-36). Six education audiovisual presentations cover such topics as burglary prevention, con games, street crime, and the use of direct deposit for social security checks. The presentations are conducted by the program staff, with active participation and cooperation of police-community relations and crime prevention departments of the police departments of Cleveland, Lakewood, and East Cleveland, Ohio. The SSSP uses trained senior citizens for these presentations to communicate effectively with their peers. In addition, younger volunteers are utilized so that there can be a mutual exchange and awareness among the youth of the security needs of senior citizens. This program also draws on the aid of letter carriers and the Neighborhood Watch program, which involves a cooperative effort with local law enforcement officials to have neighbors watch out for one another and their property in order to prevent crime and report criminal activities.

Research done by the Nova Institute in New York City in 1975 found that escort and court monitoring programs had relatively little positive effect upon reducing crime against the elderly. In fact, the technique most useful in black or Hispanic neighborhoods was relocation (Nova Institute, 1978). The bottom line is that, because of environmental and social factors, most crime problems have to be analyzed in the context of the specific area in which they occur. To be sure, the future may mandate more services and information to older persons and sensitivity training to agents in the criminal justice system to help them to adjust to this new age and sex structure of society.

Population Shifts

The Census Bureau counts people where they sleep and permanently reside. As people go to and from work, they create daytime and nighttime population shifts. During the day, Chicago, Illinois, expands by hundreds of thousands as people drive into the city to work. This causes the police to experience increased demands for specific services (for example, traffic control) during the day. Resort cities such as Las Vegas provide an example of how the population increases in the evenings, making it necessary for the casinos to hire the services of their own security staffs to handle the needs of the "swelled" population.

Geographic Areas

Another characteristic of publics is geographic areas. Different geographic areas contain people whose lifestyles produce predispositions for behavior and thus permit different kinds of programs to be established for their people. The three areas to be discussed are (1) affluent suburban areas, (2) rural small-town areas, and (3) inner-city urban areas.

Affluent Suburban Areas

These areas consist of the "bedroom" communities that develop near and around urban centers such as Washington, D.C., New York City, Los Angeles, and Montgomery County, Maryland, the wealthiest county in the United States in terms of average family income. These areas have residents who are highly educated, well paid in their occupations, and much like the upper-middle-class and upper-class people discussed earlier, who have a strong interest in public affairs and their communities. Their sophisticated, liberal ethic permeates the local criminal justice system such that in those communities, the courts, police, and corrections are comparatively well financed, functionally adequate, and, of course, liberal in outlook. Young, sophisticated, dedicated, treatment-oriented personnel are easily recruited from nearby universities to work in the criminal justice system. These affluent suburban communities can be used to develop innovative treatment programs of all kinds or to support pilot projects (Pettibone, 1973).

Rural Small-Town Areas

These comparatively unurbanized and undeveloped regions are devoted primarily to farming or fishing industries. The accepted social philosophy of such areas is conservative and individualistic, a philosophy well suited for the facts of life there. Because of the belief in basic personal self-reliance and individual responsibility, elaborate networks of social services have not been developed. The strong community sentiment in favor of low tax rates means that the criminal justice system machinery is minimally staffed, thinly spread, and conservative in orientation. Because of the low population density and family cohesiveness, these areas do not contribute heavily to prison populations. Small, community-based residential facilities can be accepted by the community. Most of the time, however, more traditional approaches are needed and emphasis is upon utilization of existing community resources or services. Mutual cooperation between the agencies and the police and courts is the usual approach (Pettibone, 1973).

Inner-City Urban Areas

Cities have heterogeneous social and economic characteristics in their various neighborhoods and ecological areas. The greatest input into the criminal justice system comes from disadvantaged, inner-city areas populated by lower-lower-class persons. Despite the high tax rates prevalent in cities, their resources are less adequate in dealing with crime and social problems than are those of suburban or rural areas. The problems are simply too great, while "everything is in short supply" (Pettibone, 1973: 6). The heterogeneous population also has a variety of viewpoints on crime and how to correct the problem. In most ethnic neighborhoods (Italian, Greek, Irish, and so on), with immigration patterns of self-reliance and hard work, the people are often very conservative in their stance. Predominantly black areas have a more liberal stance. The point is that in these areas, no program created by police, courts, or corrections will be popular and acceptable to all local communities and citizens within the cities.

One technique that has been operationalized in cities has been the identification of neighborhoods and the use of geographically organized patrols. Following neighborhood lines, the officer is better able to take into account varying needs and desires in different areas of the city (McDowell, 1975: 110). In short, being aware of geographic areas and the attitudes of the people who live therein permits one to mobilize the community support and resources needed to help communities.

SUMMARY

This chapter has discussed three other major sources of information for identifying persons and publics in a community besides walking the streets and talking to the people who live in a particular area: (1) newspapers and directories, (2) agencies, and (3) census tract data. In terms of publics, variables such as social class, population factors, and geographic areas have been shown to help predict the kinds of services different publics demand and some of the attitudes they possess for helping agents in the criminal justice system. The discussion of social class utilized five different groups to show these differences: upper, upper-middle, lower-middle, upper-lower, and lower-lower. In terms of population factors, population density, age and sex variables, and daytime/nighttime population shifts were discussed to show how these variables affect the demands for police services. The geographic areas of affluent-suburban, rural small-town, and inner-city have been discussed so that their lifestyle could be shown as a factor that determines what kinds of programs those communities will and do permit.

DISCUSSION QUESTIONS

(1) Are there other significant groups that might have an interest in defining concepts such as community and neighborhood? Could groups such as retail merchants, manufacturers, civil rights organizations, the clergy, and even victims be considered "publics"?

(2) What influence do other agencies (sometimes called boundary agencies) that interact on a daily and routine basis with police have in terms of community and public relations?

(3) Is it true that in some cities the attitude of the police is "We protect our own, and sometimes we try to protect the people"?

5

MINORITIES

In a cartoon, two ugly apes are kissing each other. The caption reads, "What you like depends on what you are used to" (Eskelin, 1980: 28). So is it with people.

At the very heart of community and public relations for agents in the criminal justice system is relations with ethnic, racial, and minority groups. A number of factors, singularly or together, have served to deter effective relations. First, there is a high degree of separation between the dominant conventional culture which produces most police officers and the minority culture. As stated in Chapter 4, many of the minority groups which interact with police may exhibit a lower-class or poverty culture. This, therefore, produces a culture shock for the agents—a personal disorientation through the loss of familiar cues.

A second factor might be that police departments in general are overwhelmingly white, male institutions. Yet they are called to interact, especially in urban areas, with large populations of lower-class and minority residents:

> The encounters between police and minority-group citizens are often dictated by cultural forces that dominate these situations and which are beyond the control of either the police or the minority group. These differing cultural perspectives predetermine the roles of each side and lead to mutually antagonistic personal contacts. The police are compelled to enforce the standards and mores of the dominant group in society, while minority groups display cultural patterns that are antiethnical to conventional norms. Within this context, they are made to be natural adversaries [Bent and Rossum, 1976: 235].

Thus, there develops a culture and historical relationship that reveals a pattern of unresolved tension. Agents in the criminal justice system often underestimate the past. They fail to realize the significance of history and the impact it has had upon minorities. To be sure, the past was not as good as the present. Take, for example, this description of police action during the riot of August 15, 1900, in New York City:

> After the classical precipitating incident of a fatal fight between a black civilian and a white policeman, rampaging crowds moved up and down Eighth and Ninth Avenues beating Negroes. Policemen swarmed over the area, cracking the heads of Negroes and doing nothing to restrain the Irish mob. Frank Moss and others carefully collected testimony concerning the police brutality and pressured the commissioners to take proper disciplinary action. In every case the commissioners refused to allow counsel for the Negro plaintiffs to cross-examine witnesses favoring the police, and whenever there was conflicting testimony they accepted the word of the police. As they explained in their report to the mayor, the police witnesses testified in an impartial manner while the witnesses for the plaintiffs "displayed a strong and bitter feeling while under examination." That the Negroes were bitter is hardly surprising seeing that the police not only did not protect them against a white mob, did not arrest any of the whites involved, but also indulged in gratuitous clubbing. The police did not stop the white rioters, they joined them [Richardson, 1970: 277].

The early history of our nation is filled with similar documented incidents of discrimination against many ethnic, racial, and religious groups. Indeed, it was not until June 1976 that the state of Missouri rescinded Executive Order Number 44, dated October 27, 1838, which called for extermination or expulsion of a Christian religious group nicknamed the Mormons. Yet in some situations, the injustice continues to the present. There are still legislators and legislation that define a "Black Panther with a gun as 'criminal,' while the KKK and members of the White Panthers organization keep their guns" (Swan, 1977: 209). The past becomes a reinforcement for present situations wherein effective channels for redress of complaints are absent. Some groups understandably conceive of the American criminal justice system as "just us."

The purpose of this chapter is to give an understanding of particular ethnic groups, which will be discussed in terms of history, special concerns, and attitudes and values. The information under those headings should give cues as to what a particular behavior might mean. Too often, minority groups have been expected to understand not only their own but also the dominant culture's worldview, while members of the dominant culture, especially those involved in legal and social service delivery, have not been compelled even to try to understand the differences, much less appreciate them. The purpose of this information, especially under the sections headed "Attitudes and Values," is to give agents in the criminal justice system some understanding so as to minimize discriminating behavior and to increase humanistic behavior patterns.

Vested interest groups will also be listed for each particular ethnic group. Agents can contact these groups in their own locality to get more pertinent information. Regional differences are extremely important. Of necessity, this chapter is written in general terms. Thus, the vested interest groups should be seen as resources for particular localities.

Before attention is given to specific groups—blacks, American Indians, Spanish-speaking Americans, and others—a short ethnic history of the United States will be presented. It is important to understand that immigration continues even today.

The inclusion of a particular group in this chapter is not intended to suggest that that group is in conflict with the police. Historically, many community-police relations textbooks have discussed only blacks. Yet, police may be called to break up family disputes among Mexican Americans or to lock up intoxicated American Indians who try, sometimes successfully, to commit suicide. The material in this chapter in connection with the information in other chapters should help agents deal more effectively with minority groups and help these groups to develop more working relationships with criminal justice agencies.

INTRODUCTION

The history of the United States of America is a history of racial and ethnic groups. From 1502 to 1860, 9.5 million Africans were involuntarily transported to the New World. Of that number, more than 6 million were brought to the American colonies.

> Between 1780 and 1810 about as many slaves were brought into the United States as had been introduced in the previous 160 years. The United States, along with Great Britain, passed legislation prohibiting slave trades in 1807. By the time of Emancipation, almost 60 years later, only 1 percent of the black population in this country was foreign-born [Hraba, 1979: 9].

From 1820 until 1960, 82 percent of the total immigration into this country was by Europeans. The immigrants from Northern and Western Europe came earlier (1830-1860) than those from Southern and Eastern Europe (1890-1920). German and Irish immigration peaked between 1840 and 1860. Scandinavians immigrated after 1860 and settled primarily in the Midwest. From 1890 to 1920, immigrants from Italy, Poland, and Russia (Jews) exceeded previous figures to the point that quota acts were passed in the 1920s (Hraba, 1979: 9-12).

In addition to Europeans, more than 1 million Asians immigrated to the United States between 1820 and 1960. Of that number, the Chinese and Japanese are the two largest Asian immigrant groups and are best known for their efforts in the West, building railroads in the 1860s and an agrarian empire in California in the 1870s and 1880s. After World War II, many Asian immigrants became war brides (Hraba, 1979: 12).

Mexican Americans are both an indigenous people and an immigrant group. By indigenous, it is meant that they, like the American Indian, were living in parts of the Southwest in the middle of the nineteenth century, when the United States assumed control of that region. Legal immigration from 1910 to 1960 numbered 1,110,652 (Hraba, 1979: 12-13).

Mexicans remain unrevealed as the largest body of illegal immigrants. Other illegal immigrants have come from other North American and Asian countries. The estimated guess of the current net population of illegal aliens living in the United States is close to 6 million. "The full impact of both legal and illegal migrants on the cost of America's societal programs is difficult to estimate, but in many local geographic areas it is substantial" (McLennan and Lovell, 1981: 42).

America's latest newcomers are more apt to be refugees, mostly females, to have higher skills than immigrants before them, and to come from Third World nations (Reimers, 1981: 1). Another feature of present-day immigrants has been the recent flood of "boat people"— Vietnamese, Cuban, and Haitian refugees who have come to the United States due to political situations in their own countries. In August 1980, the federal government reported that there were about 380,000 Indochinese refugees and 120,000 Cubans (Reimers, 1981: 11). Yet this has not been done through formal channels and has been in excess of the number already admitted through the formal quota systems. The large numbers of refugees supersaturated various reception areas and, thereby, have caused chaos (McLennan and Lovell, 1981: 12).

Today, besides dealing with the normal problem of immigration and naturalization, it is important to develop a policy concerning illegal aliens and refugees. Immigration becomes an issue for the Congress and the public, so that they must decide what limits need to be established—how many immigrants will be admitted—and what criteria will be used to select them. Social, economic, and moral questions will have to be examined in formulating such an immigration policy (Reimers, 1981: 12). One thing is certain: Our country will continue to have immigrants who represent a way of life different from the one each one of us possesses. How groups react to one another has been the study of sociologists, who suggest three theories of ethnic and race relations.

THEORIES OF ETHNIC AND RACE RELATIONS[1]

For various reasons (survival, intermarriage, extramarital affairs, and so on), many cultural, ethnic, and racial groups have developed or merged into a newer, different kind of society. As a result, early sociologists recognized that there were no pure races such as Caucasians, Negroid, and Mongoloid. Thus, these social investigators turned their attention away from biological differences and focused on group relations.[2] From that sociological literature on ethnic and race relations in American society come three schools of thought: assimilationism, ethnic pluralism, and ethnic conflict.

Assimilationism

Assimilationist theorists—such as Robert Park and Louis Wirth, of the early Chicago School of Sociology, and Gunnar Myrdal, a European sociologist who studied prejudice in America—contended that our society assimilates social ethnic groups. From this mixture of different nationalities and cultural diversities comes a new culture called "American." Sometimes referred to as the "melting pot," America is viewed as a place where folk groups, through the process of modernization and Westernization, are assimilated into an "achievement-oriented, rationalized and impersonal social relationship of the modern, industrial-bureaucratic order" (Mitzger, 1971: 635). In this school of thought, scholars view folk groups as being absorbed into a modern society. Children are sent to a unitary school system which perpetuates rational thinking and mass attitudes and values, and eventually these children are dispersed throughout a broad range of occupations. To these scholars, assimilation is the result of societal modernization. That is to say, groups come to share a common culture as the result of industrialization, occupational diversification, urbanization, and the spread of mass education and literacy. In addition to this element of a common culture, assimilation means that ethnic and racial groups have equal access to the opportunity structure of a society.

The assimilation perspective—as exemplified by Park, who studied race relations in such metropolitan cities as Chicago—says that struggle and strife are resolved through human communication. This leads to accommodation and, later, assimilation. What competition there is, is settled through mutual understanding and rules. Louis Wirth's *The Ghetto* (1928), for instance, shows how the natural history of Jewish assimilation in Chicago occurred.

The assimilationists' perspective gives fuel to the fire that someday this society really will be a giant melting pot. The assimilationists have helped us to understand that assimilation is often realized in terms of social class mobility. Thus, Chinese and Japanese Americans have assimilated to a far greater degree than have blacks. The assimilationists also argue that when there were both biological and cultural traits of a group that were different from the larger society, assimilation would be slow and perhaps, at times, painful.

Others argue that assimilationists have lumped too many groups together, for American Indians, Asian Americans, black Americans, and Mexican Americans are as divergent from one another as they are divergent from white immigrant groups. American Indians are far less assimilated than blacks, even though both groups share the experience of color prejudice (Hraba, 1979: 58). Thus, for further understanding, it is important to look to the perspective presented by ethnic pluralism.

Ethnic Pluralism

Whereas in assimilationism our society is likened to a single melting pot wherein diverse groups, like beef and vegetables, are placed together and over a period of time, with heat (conflict), become a delicious stew, pluralists contend that there are many melting pots. Some ethnic groups fuse together in one pot, while others fuse together in another. Each melting pot is thereby distinct from others. In this way, then, instead of disappearing or melting into all other groups, ethnic and racial groups become new forms and expressions, updated with societal modernization. A national, ethnic, or racial group, in either occupational composition or residential dispersion, perceives itself as a group of people who think, feel, and act in common, holding a set of traditions not shared by others with whom they are in contact. A group may be *cultural* (such as the Amish) or it may be *structural* (the group restricts social interaction or the use of ethnic identity in open and free exchange). Studies done in major metropolitan areas show that even though certain ethnic groups are residents of a city, they maintain a social distance among themselves. Social interaction in the churches, clubs, business establishments, taverns, and recreational areas of the neighborhood, and even membership in the juvenile gangs, is based upon racial or ethnic identity with people of their own kind.

Ethnic pluralism is especially noticeable when new immigrants turn to one another for help. Whenever possible, immigrants have organized with others from the same village or region of the old country to create a "little Italy" or a "little Greece" or a "Chinatown." Vecoli, in 1970, identified twenty "little Italies" in Chicago alone (see Hraba, 1979: 74). Communication habits and clothing styles also help maintain ethnic boundaries.

Some ethnic pluralists believe that ethnic pluralism for white Americans is not defined by nationality groups as much as it has developed into a subsociety or subculture based upon religion. Some theorists argue that our national heritage of societal tolerance for religious but not national diversity is the reason that there has not been full assimilation.

Recently, some ethnic and racial groups have revived themselves due to the ethnic and racial realities of American politics. As Hraba (1979: 87) states:

> Subjective ethnic identities were rekindled and evolved in many instances into the objective forms of political interest groups. Here in the United States and elsewhere in the world, ethnicity has become a legitimate and efficacious way to make resource claims in the modern state. So long as it plays a role in resource competition in American society, ethnicity as a subjective consciousness of kind will endure here. And it is always possible that ethnicity will again take more objective and social forms, particularly that of the political interest group.

Ethnic Conflict

According to this third theory, competition and conflict among ethnic and racial groups increase in the process of societal modernization. Instead of the demise of folk groups and assimilation into a mass society, groups struggle with and exploit one another. This theoretical perspective is based upon the key idea that there are limited materials and symbolic resources. Thus, a struggle over the rewards or resources of a society or over social values is inevitable. Intergroup conflict between white settlers and the American Indians, between early Protestant and Catholic groups and Mormons, and between blacks and whites are some instances in American history.

According to this perspective, powerful groups limit the access of subordinate groups to societal resources such as wealth, power, and prestige. Power, not human need, is viewed as the necessary element that will determine the distribution of wealth in modern society. As such, power is not always based upon numbers. More so than not, it also includes the control of other power resources and the capacity to mobilize these resources:

> Racial and ethnic stratification in the labor market has been a recurrent phenomenon in American history, and many immigrant groups have shared in these experiences. Blacks were excluded from the textile mills in the post-Reconstructionist South and remained in agrarian labor pools un-

der the white planters. In the past century, Chinese were forced out of mining and all sorts of desirable jobs on the West Coast, and later, in the twentieth century, Japanese immigrants had some of the same experiences there. Mexican farm labor duplicated in the Southwest some of the dimensions of the black experience in the South. In the Northeast, Poles worked in factories under Irish foremen, who in turn worked under Anglo managers. It was the Irish who had been the common laborers in the nineteenth century, and so concentrated were they in unskilled labor that a joke of the era asked why the wheelbarrow was man's greatest invention, to which Americans answered, because it had taught the Irish to walk on their hind legs. Such has been the character of the ethnic and racial stratification of labor in this nation [Hraba, 1979: 109-110].

Along with power and intergroup competition came ethnocentrism—a belief that one's own group is better than another. Spin-offs of this element might be racism and sexism. Thus, it is not custom that keeps people "in their places"; it is coercion, the threat of violence or of losing one's job. There is a lot of evidence in our society to support the idea that ethnic or racial groups struggle with one another and that a stratification occurs that keeps certain persons in low-paying jobs.

These three theories—assimilationism, ethnic pluralism, and conflict theory—help to give a fuller understanding of American ethnicity. Each theory complements the others or makes up for something the others lack. In fact, some cultural and ethnic groups might have, throughout American history, experienced all three. The American Indians, at first, were examples of ethnic pluralism, with many different tribes and nations. Then the white settlers wanted and/or needed the land for western settlements. The conflict that arose nearly annihilated the American Indian. American scholars of Indian populations at the time Columbus arrived in the Western Hemisphere, in 1492, place the figure at nearly 10 million. At the turn of this century, the estimate was 235,000 ("The Indian and the Frontier," 1973: 45). The scope of this tragedy was the result of warfare—both combat and epidemic diseases. Indians were killed off by epidemics of smallpox, bubonic plague, typhus, influenza, malaria, measles, yellow fever, and other diseases. The blankets at the Indian trading posts were covered with strains of the virus and bacteria, so that when Indians traded for blankets to keep themselves warm, they sealed their own fate. Of those that did survive and lived on reservations, a process of assimilation took place. Some Indians felt that although they were red on the outside, they had become white on the inside. Through the civil rights movement of the 1960s, the Indians created an ethnic awareness with "red power" that has led to a pluralism and an awareness of pride and heritage of specific Indian tribes. Thus, one can see how each of these three theories highlights a different segment of the larger process of social change.

MINORITY GROUPS

In this section, each ethnic, racial, or other minority group will be discussed in terms of its history, special concerns, attitudes and values, and vested interest groups.

Blacks

History

Africans were brought to the New World from 1502 to 1860 (Hraba, 1979: 255). During the early part of those three centuries, many worked in sugar production or in mines in Mexico and Brazil. The first Africans, in what is now called America, were brought first to Virginia in 1619 and later to other colonies. These black persons were like many of the whites—indentured servants. To gain his freedom, a servant had to work for a master for a specified period of time; others became free men through conversion to Christianity.

Africans were brought to the frontier for one fundamental reason: to replace Native Americans as laborers (Hraba, 1979: 254). The Europeans had tried to use the natives as agriculturalists, but found that they were not accustomed to hard, continuous labor. In addition, they were a security threat in that they could ally with free natives in retaliatory raids against planters.

Although costly and demanding importation across a great distance, the African slaves proved to be an attractive alternative to native labor. There were several reasons for this. Paramount to this discussion is the fact that slaves from West Africa were skillful in agriculture and cultivation. Politically, the West African tribes were unable to stop the European powers. In addition, powers such as the British, French, Dutch, Portuguese, and Spanish fanned intertribal hostility with alcohol and other inducements and took slaves out by the thousands.

It may seem odd, but so long as African labor remained in Africa it was of little use to Europeans. African labor had to be exported to be of use to

Europeans elsewhere in the world. At least this was the case until the middle of the nineteenth century, when European powers eventually colonized much of Africa and could use African labor at home. At this time the slave trade finally stopped [Hraba, 1979: 255].

The British, for example, were able to finance their Industrial Revolution through the famous "triangle" operation. Britain shipped finished products to Africa in trade for slaves. The slaves were shipped to the New World in trade for raw materials, and the raw materials were then shipped home to England to be made into finished products. Needless to say, England made a profit from each leg of the triangle. This operation continued until the United States became an independent nation.

What had been happening in the newly developing United States was that Northern states were abolishing the practice of slavery by law, while the more industrial Southern states, which were largely agricultural, still depended upon slave labor. By the 1830s, the practice of slavery was under severe attack. Historically, much was said and written about this practice, and there was a lot of debate and controversy. Some critics, for example, argued that slavery was inhumane and cruel: "With the whip sadistic white masters and their overseers coerced slaves into labor and often forced sexual attention on black women. Black bodies and souls alike were abused in the process (Hraba, 1979: 256). Others viewed slaves as property and insisted that they were not regularly brutalized or sexually molested in any systematic way; if there were examples of physical punishment, it was nothing more than what a father might do occasionally to correct his child.

Later, a doctrine of racial superiority was used to justify continued subjugation. "Negroes" were considered as biologically inferior. Since they could never attain a white person's I.Q., it was proper for Negroes to be viewed as property with no rights, which the white person was bound to respect. In 1857, the famous Dred Scott decision of the U.S. Supreme Court supported this argument. Scott, a slave, had been taken into a territory that prohibited slavery and thus considered himself a free man under the rules of the Missouri Compromise. The Court claimed that Congress had erred and that the Compromise was unconstitutional. The Court argued that Congress had no right to enact a law in the territories of the United States which would deprive people of their property.

Prior to the Civil War, there was a class of free blacks who represented approximately 11 percent of the black population in this country. These people were educated and had family stability and economic autonomy.

Some were barbers, shoemakers, butchers, and/or controlled the building trades.

The descendants of this class, along with the children of black families in the South who were fortunate enough to have acquired land or a profession after Emancipation, made up the bulk of black college students well into the present century. The "talented tenth," as they have been called, has been moving closer than the black masses to intergroup inclusion in and evolutionary convergence with the larger society [Hraba, 1979: 263].

Needless to say, the slavery issue culminated in the Civil War. The slaves were emancipated and federal troops were used to maintain order. Negroes who had gained equal status in the law in the South soon lost more of those rights during the period of Reconstruction. Southern leaders made a compromise in 1877 that led to carpet baggers and Federal troops withdrawing. By the 1890s, the Southern society had developed into a two-caste system with whites having power. The Plessy v. Ferguson decision of the U.S. Supreme Court in 1896 sanctioned the "separate but equal" policy. Thus, Negroes were virtually barred from all white institutions. Even some rest rooms and water fountains were labeled as "colored only." The significance of the inequality of educational services offered to blacks and whites would later manifest itself when the nation's labor needs moved toward mental-oriented, white-collar work. It was not until 1954 that the U.S. Supreme Court, in Brown v. Board of Education of Topeka, reversed the "separate but equal" decision.

In 1910, almost 90 percent of blacks in the United States lived in the South; after World War I, however, labor shortages beckoned many to the North. Patterns of "Negro segregation" and barriers to opportunity were present in the North as well. There, the migration of blacks brought competition between the races for jobs, housing, and the use of public recreational facilities. Thus, many cities became, as McLemore (1980: 279) says, "powder kegs" of racial resentment and unrest:

Lynchings, especially of blacks by whites, were a source of great concern. Although the actual number of lynchings was somewhat lower between 1910 and 1920 than in the two previous decades, the circumstances under which they occurred and the publicity they received led to more open and angry denunciations by black spokesmen than in the past. Many lynchings were conducted in an especially sadistic way and in a carnival atmosphere. Some victims were tortured and burned; some newspapers issued invitations to whites to come to witness a lynching or a burning.

The period before and during World War II was not much better. Although the United States was fighting against fascism and the doctrine of white supremacy as a matter of official principle, it had a difficult time putting policy into action or practice:

> The way the military services were organized supplied daily examples of the discrepancy. Throughout the military services, Jim Crow practices were common. And since many military training camps were in the South, black servicemen faced segregation when they left the camps. They were frequently in danger of physical assault not only by local citizens but by officers of the law as well. For instance, a black soldier was shot in Little Rock, Arkansas, because he would not tip his hat and say "sir" to a policeman. Another black soldier was shot by two police officers because he had taken a bus seat reserved for a white in Beaumont, Texas (Rustin, 1971: 235). In Centerville, Mississippi, a sheriff obligingly shot a black soldier in the chest merely because a white MP asked him to (Milneer, 1968: 419) [McLemore, 1980: 287].

After World War II, many changes occurred. The most profound for blacks was the movement off the land in the South and into the cities. By 1970, for example, only 52 percent of black Americans were living in the South, while 55 percent of black Americans were living in our nation's central cities. This migration of blacks to the urban North and West meant that they were included in industrial blue-collar threads and white-collar work. That led, of course, to improved living conditions, health, wealth, and education. Black art, theater, literature, and music were pursued professionally. Rock music, for example, contains a distinctly black cultural motif. This music has been played and listened to by millions of youth of all classes and ethnic groups and in all regions of the United States. Music, along with sports and the other performing arts, are good examples of how black folk traditions are being assimilated into American culture (Hraba, 1979: 277-283).

The civil rights movement of the 1960s increased the opportunities for equal housing, education, and employment. Yet that does not mean that all is equal. Even after 1940, black unemployment continued to exceed that of whites. It is the black youths—who live in the inner city and have few or limited skills and/or little access to industries in the suburbs—who have the highest unemployment rates. In addition, there has always been an absence of black proprietors and entrepreneurs as well as business managers, public officials, and elected politicians (Hraba, 1979: 287). Granted, the picture is somewhat changing. The essence of the history of black people, however, is one of people laboring for others.

The most recent trend of the convergence of some black Americans with the larger society has been with the mobility of young adults and women. Working black women now make 90 percent of the income of their white counterparts (Hraba, 1979: 288). Obviously, it is the better educated blacks who are able to accomplish this task.

The 1980 annual report of the National Urban League argued that blacks never recovered from the recession of the 1970s. Thus, the current recession/depression will only widen the black-white gap. If there are any gains in the 1980s, this report says that they will be largely dependent on new job opportunities for female heads of families, who make up more than a third of all black families (Jordan, 1980).

In short, this means that there is a black middle class which will probably keep abreast of changes within the occupational structure. There is also the black poor. This means that even among blacks, there is division of classes. These poor include black women on welfare and unemployed black males. Given the current discrepancy between skills and education and the evolving technology in the nation, there is little reason to predict that these poor blacks will be assimilated into American society. There would have to be political decisions dealing with education, employment, welfare, and income redistribution in order for that to occur.

Special Concerns

As voiced through the leaders and spokespersons, one of the greatest concerns these people have is for the elimination of discrimination, with its faulty racist beliefs. One of these is the idea that some races are physically superior to others. Support for this myth comes from some of the differences in rates of selected disease. For example, blacks in the United States have traditionally had higher rates than whites of tuberculosis, infant mortality, and sickle-cell anemia:

Sickle-cell anemia is a genetic, blood-connected factor that illustrates the dubious relationship of blood type to race. This disease is frequent among American blacks and West African areas from which the slaves came. However, it is also frequent among nonnegroid populations in Greece, southern India, and other areas of the world. In fact, the sickle-cell strain in the past was found in areas of the world that had high rates of malaria, and it appears to have been an adaptive response to that disease. Knowledge of blood-related traits may help to understand human disease, but caution is in order [when] suggesting racial interpretations [Davis, 1978: 90-91].

Differences in occupation, income, housing, sanitation, nutrition, medical care, and education are better predictors of diseases and infant mortality than is race.

A second erroneous belief is that some races are mentally superior to others. The fact is that I.Q. tests are not culturally unbiased. In fact, the Stanford-Binet (the most widely used I.Q. test), was standardized for white, middle-class Americans. As learning opportunities improve, so does I.Q. Even longitudinal studies (studies done over time) show that people can increase their I.Q. if they keep mentally alert, active, and stimulated. As long as people erroneously believe that intelligence is hereditary, however, they will do little to effect changes in the environment.

A third erroneous belief which is used to discriminate against blacks is the idea that a race causes a culture. This leads to the notion that a particular ethnic or racial group is naturally prone to criminality, sexual looseness, or dishonest business practices. However, take an issue such as drug use and abuse. Studies of victimization and self-report studies show that many of our nation's youth, regardless of racial or ethnic background, have taken or are abusing drugs. A Korean baby who is adopted by a midwestern Kansas family will internalize the midwestern culture. The carrier of race is genes, but *the carrier of culture is communication*.

A fourth erroneous belief is that racial mixing lowers biological quality. "The genetic mixing of human groups has been going on a very long time, and certainly it's a myth that European national and subracial groups were genetically pure types not so many generations ago. There is no scientific proof that racial mixing leads to lower or higher biological quality" (Davis, 1978: 96).

These erroneous beliefs make up what some people call "racism," a set of beliefs about racial groups used to justify institutional discrimination. In addition, these and many other ideas are used to justify interracial violence in general, and, in particular, rigorous, unnecessary frisking, verbal abuse, and other forms of aggressive force by agents in the criminal justice system.

Attitudes and Values

In this section, certain key attitudes or values will be discussed so that they might act as cues and provide agents with a greater understanding of their clientele.

Blacks value their families. Some scholars (McLemore, 1980: 302) say that they have stronger kinship bonds than do whites:

> Though in no way an exhaustive listing, the special characteristics of black families are identified as: (1) they are comprised of several individual households, with the family definition and lines of authority and support transcending or going beyond any one household unit which comprises the "family"; (2) they are structurally expanding and diminishing in response to external conditions (elasticity); (3) they have a child-centered system (the general organizational purpose of the family focuses on, if not requires, the presence of children); (4) they have a close network of relationship between families not necessarily related by blood (family networking); (5) they have flexible and interchangeable role definitions and performance (in child rearing a clear distinction is maintained between role definition [sex-linked] and the role performance [sexless]); and (6) they have multiple parenting and interfamilial consensual adoptions [Nobles, 1978: 687].

This means that both the young child and the elderly are valued. Friends who are older might serve the role of aunt or uncle. Through slavery, black women had to raise the children of the mistress who might look more black than white. The black woman who had been raped by a white man, during those times, had to raise the child. There were no abortions. To be sure, black women learned to raise the rejected. Thus, today, an unwed, black teenager is more prone to have and raise a child than she is to have an abortion.

In black families, in addition, there is a strong dimension of helping others in crisis. Besides the strong kinship pattern, there emerges the blood or informal adoption of sisters and brothers. When two women feel that they are communicating with each other and sharing feelings, they may call each other "sister" even though they are not biologically related; it is a spiritual rather than biological sisterhood that binds them together.

Some early researchers show the American black family as a consequence of slavery and of American culture which has been characterized by injustice and inhumanity (as evidenced by varying degrees of discrimination in jobs; segregation in housing, education, and health services; and differential processing through the criminal justice system). The American culture was the same refiner's fire that was used with other ethnic groups (Irish, Polish, and so on). Frazier (1932-1937), in using the sociological methods employed by such scholars as Park, from the Chicago School, found that blacks living in the inner city were highly disorganized, economically unstable, demoralized, and headed by females (Mathis, 1978: 669).

It took research in the 1960s and 1970s in both sociological and urban studies areas to correct this historical bias. Thus, later studies showed that female-headed black families are in a minority. What matriarchal families there were, as in middle-class white culture, were not produced by the values of the community but rather were the result of social-structural factors that caused black males to abandon their role (Mathis, 1978: 670).

The most important element of this attitude toward the family is the protectiveness of family members toward children and each other. Black mothers' protection of their sons has caused many a rookie officer to learn a hard lesson. Remember what was said about previous brutality at the hands of police early in our history? Well, many blacks still fear that is going on. Thus, large numbers of blacks, usually a family, will congregate to prevent an officer from mistreating someone they know and love. In one case, a black female who had been raped reported it to a sexual assault center. When the victim advocate came and discussed the options with the victim, the rape victim wanted to go elsewhere to make the report to the police. She knew that if she gave her report from her home to a uniformed patrol person, everyone in the neighborhood would see the police car and come to see what had happened. She did not want that, so she went elsewhere to make the police report (personal experience, Wichita, Kansas).

In short, black families are characterized by extended family structures and networks which give aid and support. Familial relationships need not be those of blood. "Aunts" might not really be aunts. Boyfriends often take on the role of father (Schulz, 1970). In fact, research even among lower-class black men and women in a large urban public housing project collected over a period of three and one-half years (Schulz, 1970) showed that many men were concerned for and supportive of the women (contrary to the popular image of the lower-class male). "The extended family pattern continues to be a viable cultural component for the emotional well-being of blacks at all economic levels, even when middle-class status has been maintained over several generations" (McAdoo, 1978: 775).

Blacks value religion. Martin Luther King, Jr., was only one of the prominent ministers in the civil rights movement. His famous speech, "I have a dream," was not for blacks alone but for all people. It was a dream of an American society in which there was to be no hunger or meanness, a society in which everyone could live his or her life to the best of his or her God-given talents. Part of the emphasis of religion is a retention of an

African attitude, an attitude based on a belief system that envisioned everything in the universe as endowed with the Supreme Force. Since all things are endowed with this same Supreme Force, then all things, they reason, must be interconnected or interdependent (Nobles, 1978: 684).

Black churches serve their communities in more than simply religious ways. In fact, the black church is a social institution in itself. It is no wonder that many of the social and welfare needs of blacks for generations have been met through the churches. Besides the black Baptist churches, there are the Black Muslims. The Lost Nation of Islam was launched in the 1930s. One of its early teachers was Elijah Muhammad, and one of its famous converts, Malcolm X. Although religion and politics were intermingled, religion for the Black Muslim was paramount. The religion maintains a moral code which forbids the use of tobacco and drugs, extramarital sexual relations, racial intermarriage, dancing, laziness, lying, and a host of other things. Although the number of people who are officially members of the Black Muslim organization is unknown, there is wide acceptance and respect for the Muslims' high standards and strict discipline. This religion has helped to revitalize the lives of many people who previously had given up in the face of seemingly overwhelming troubles. In particular, the Muslims have been successful in the rehabilitation of ex-convicts and drug addicts (McLemore, 1980: 283).

Blacks value education. What hampers their attainment of it is that their learning style is more affective as opposed to instrumental, and many middle-class teachers are more prone to teach in an instrumental style. A second drawback comes from their speaking style—"Black English." Black English is said to be used by about 80 percent of black Americans in informal conversation. It includes putting endings on some words while leaving off the endings on others, misusing grammar (with phrases such as "he be right back" and substituting the "f" sound for "th" to produce words such as "wif" (with) or "worf" (worth). Some of these words, originally used solely by blacks in the ghettos, have worked their way into white slang. Two of the best known examples are "rip off" (steal) and "rap" (talk). What is most important for agents in the criminal justice system is that this speech pattern can be misinterpreted. Police mistake the high-pitched, excited sounds of blacks in conversation to signify a fight. Just as one learns some phrases in Italian when one expects to travel in Italy, an agent might want to learn some Black English.

Blacks value law and order. The black cop—"black in blue"—is a person caught in the middle (Alex, 1969).

Finally, blacks value material goods as well. Blacks who have not been able to purchase their own homes put money into cars. Their cars become important to them, showing their style and personality, just as a person's home reveals something about him or her.

The values of family, religion, education, law and order, and materialism represent universal black values. Values and attitudes are the forerunners of behavior, and knowing these values should help agents in the criminal justice system. Caution has to be exercised, as with any group, because sometimes there is dissonance between what a group says they believe and what they actually do.

Vested Interest Groups

Throughout the years, there have been several important organizations that have been in the forefront of black issues. Some of these groups, such as the Black Panther Party of the late 1960s, have been more radical or militant than other groups. The purpose of this section is not to relate the historical developments of specific national organizations, but rather to identify specific organizations that may be of benefit to agents in the criminal justice system. These organizations might be contacted for information or even cooperation for a specific program.

The National Association for the Advancement of Colored People (NAACP) was organized in 1909. Some say the NAACP is a spiritual descendant of the abolitionist movement, for they argue against the "ever-growing expression" and for free public education for everyone, including blacks. NAACP members, including a group of white liberals, have called on Congress and the executive office to enforce strictly the Constitution's provisions for civil rights. Thus, the NAACP throughout the years has adopted a legal and legislative strategy (McLemore, 1980: 279).

Another important organization consisting of both blacks and non-blacks started in 1911 as the National Urban League. "The Urban League has always been considered much more conservative than 'protest' organizations like the NAACP" (McLemore, 1980: 319n12).

Both the NAACP and the Urban League have national headquarters with regional or state offices in strategic locations to help meet the needs of blacks. Other groups that have a history in the black movement and that might have local community representation are the Congress of Racial Equality (CORE), the Southern Christian Leadership Conference (SCLC), and the Student Non-Violent Coordinating Committee (SNCC). In addition, religious groups, both Protestant and Muslim, can be consulted. On college and university campuses, there are black faculty who might help, as well as black sororities and fraternities. For criminal justice information, consult the National Organization of Black Law Enforcement Executives (NOBLE) and the National Association of Blacks in Criminal Justice (NABCJ).

American Indians/Native Americans

It is most inaccurate to speak generically of the American Indian. There never really has been a characteristic single Indian culture, as so often fictionalized by novelists or portrayed in the movies. Rather, American Indians need to be viewed as a nation of tribes. "There are 467 recognized Indian tribes and bands in this country with populations ranging from less than 100 to more than 100,000 [Navajo] nations, and speaking some 200 different tribal dialects" (French, 1980: 75-76).

The tribes inhabited the forests, plains, deserts, and mountain ranges of the Americas. Thus, there is a wide range of cultural patterns in their social structures and political organizations. Historically, some tribes, such as the Iroquois, were nominally democratic; others, such as the Comanche and the Cheyenne, were considered autocratic. Some tribes stressed competitiveness between individuals; others, like the Zuni, emphasized cooperation and communal sharing. The Navaho fought only in reprisal; the Ute and Apache, on the other hand, glorified warfare.

Despite these differences, there was a psychocultural orientation that these people possessed in common. In their traditional heritage there was a cultural philosophy or way of viewing the world which affected their interpersonal and environmental relationships:

> Violence during aboriginal times, for all intents and purposes, was directed toward other tribes and bands who were considered to exist outside the realm of the particular tribe's world-orientation. This is why so many Indian tribal names translate to mean "the principal people." Prior to white contact, the "harmony ethic" seemed sufficiently strong enough to maintain not only an Indian/nature balance but an intertribal balance as well. Massive social and personal disorganization and disruption were a direct consequence of white contact and conflict [French, 1980: 76].

The purpose of this section will be to provide a general understanding of these tribes, who shared in the fact that the conquering whites markedly influenced their ways. This material should give insight into why Indians have the highest violent crime of any racial group in the United States. The conditions of the reservation and the urban ghetto are often used to rationalize the violence-related deaths, including suicide, which occur there. The purpose of the history section is to show how the Indians got to the reservations and urban ghettos. Through this understanding, then, when agents come into contact with Indians, they may have a greater sensitivity to the social and historical conditions that placed Indians where they are, and perhaps the agents will be less likely to blame the victim.

History

In the days before the conquests, it is estimated that more than 1 million Indians occupied the territory now comprising the United States and Canada. In total, there may have been as many as 20 to 40 million Indians living in the Western Hemisphere. These indigenous people came to be called Indians by the Europeans who came to North America. Christopher Columbus, upon reaching Haiti, remarked that "they are . . . generous . . . of anything they have, if it be asked, for, they never say no, but do rather invite the person to accept it, and show as much lovingness as though they would give their hearts" (Hraba, 1979: 210).

The early Spaniards, some 250 years ago, seeking to extort riches from the Indians, were the first to mistreat and abuse them. The Dutch, the British, and the French continued the abuse and coerced the Indians into retreating from their lands as the three superpowers fought one another for control of the land. The British, in the Royal Proclamation of 1763, recognized the Indians as the rightful owners of the land in the Americas. Land, according to that proclamation, was not to be taken from the Indians except in fair exchange (Hraba, 1979: 213).

Needless to say, best intentions gave way to greed. As the frontier moved westward, the new American government became the unrivaled power in the land. Indians believed in symbolically sharing the land; the early settlers believed in European traditions of private property and exclusive ownership of land. Conflict arose. The new American government vacillated between attempts at bilateral negotiations with members of the so-called "sovereign Indian nations" and outright massacre and removal. In some cases, military force was used to make Indians move to a specific location. In 1838, the Cherokee were driven from their homes in North Carolina and Georgia, for example. The military helped move them to Oklahoma. One-third of the Cherokee died en route.

What emerged was an exclusionary policy. With the actions of President Andrew Jackson, the Indian Removal Act of 1830 began an era of removal of Indians from white settlements to isolation on reservations. Fraudulent treaties, removal, and allotment were three powerful tools used to deplete the Indians of land, water, minerals, and other resources. Some of those actions, such as the treaties, are still being contested in federal courts today.

In 1924, the Sixty-Eighth Congress gave authority to the Secretary of the Interior to issue certificates of citizenship to Indians who were born within the territorial limits, and the status of the Indian changed from an "enemy hostile" to a "ward."

The reservations were grossly inadequate in health, medical, educational, and other human services. The result was that Indians continued to die. In 1860, there were only about 340,000. In 1910, there were some 220,000. Indians were killed off by catastrophic diseases in the form of epidemics of smallpox, bubonic plague, typhus, influenza, malaria, measles, and yellow fever. In fact, smallpox virus was placed on the blankets to be sold at the reservations. In addition to these diseases, the Europeans brought weeds, plants, rats, insects, domestic animals, liquor, and a new technology to alter the Indian life and ecological balance of the entire continent. In some places, life was so terrible that there was mass abstinence from sexual activity if not mass infanticide, so that children would not be born into that mess. The reservation was the worst of all worlds for several generations.

Regardless of how Indians were being treated on the reservations, the American government expected them to fulfill obligations to their country (such as fighting for democracy during World War II). Chief Elbert Garee, Cataba Indian chief, related that when he was an engineer on the Navaho reservation from 1933 to 1939, he was asked, along with many other young men with above-average education, to volunteer for the army. As a scout in a patrol of twelve Navaho men in the Forty-Fifth Infantry Division, his task was to go before the front lines—sometimes as much as sixty miles—to help the American troops in Sicily, Italy, and France. In total, there were 25,000 Indian men and women who served in the armed forces. Yet, most notable were the scouts, who used their native language (Navaho) as a battlefield code that could not be broken by the enemy either in Europe or in the Pacific.

In the early 1950s, the American government began a process of termination with the hope of getting rid of the reservation. The failure of the termination process resulted in many Indians leaving the reservation for the urban ghetto. In addition, in the mid-1950s there were federal programs to leave the older generation on the reservations and to relocate the younger Indians to the cities, where educational and job prospects were supposedly better. The Indian Vocational Training Act (1956) began the process and continues today under the Direct Employment and Adult Vocational Training Program. Also, "Native Americans found that once again a federally sponsored Indian program had led to false hopes by replacing rural poverty with that of urban poverty and despair" (Hraba, 1979: 82).

It is no wonder, then, that a special movement emerged: Pan Indianism. The American Indian Movement attempted to address the issue of being torn between two contravening cultural expectations without the possibility of fully belonging to either. The movement wanted more autonomy and the right to cultural survival. To bring national attention to this issue, the leaders of the movement created a "Trail of Broken Treaties" which culminated in November of 1972 with the hand-delivering of "Twenty Points" to the White House. This document was the American Indian Movement's "Declaration of Independence," and was predicated upon the reality that the Native Americans had been ill prepared for a viable social position either in the traditional culture or in the majority society. Some people argue that the high rates of alcoholism and violence are a direct result of the high tension and ambiguous situation confronting marginal Indians (French, 1980; Forslund, 1974).

In addition,

> when young Indians learn of their rich, yet unobtainable, past heritage and the role the majority society played in white/Indian relations, they often feel an inner rage and a personal ambivalence that forces them to withdraw further from the majority society or to join an antiestablishment (rebellion) or anti-tribal movement (the AIM phenomenon) [Hraba, 1979: 83].

Besides the previously mentioned social problems, even today Native Americans have the highest rates of infant mortality (American Indian Policy Review Commission, 1977), educational dropout (Havinghurst, 1978), therapy dropout (Sue et al., 1978), unemployment (Stanley and Thomas, 1978), and child adoption and foster placement (Report on Federal, State and Tribal Jurisdiction, 1976). They also have the lowest income (Stanley and Thomas, 1978), life expectancy (American Indian Review Commission, 1976), and number of trained professionals (Dauphinais, 1979). From these statistics, even today, it easy to conclude that the basic social, economic, and psychological resources have not been operationalized for Indians.

Special Concerns

Three legal codes—federal, state, and tribal—apply to Indian offenses. Laws from all three codes may be involved in various phases of the same case. The difficulties and complexities that emerge from the overlap of these three areas are beyond the scope of this text, yet it is important to realize the complexities and injustices that do occur.

Another special concern is treatment by police. Although the Native American is entitled to be free from discrimination by officials and public organizations, the Indian is, in some places, treated harshly by law enforcement officials. In the twin cities of St. Paul and Minneapolis, it was once customary for the police to harass Indians on the weekend. Their arrest rate for drunkenness in these cities was far out of proportion to that of other groups in the metropolitan area. In a move to counter this discrimination, some of the Indians in Minneapolis joined together to form an Indian patrol to watch the actions of the police in the Indian section of town. They followed police cars around the area and acted as witnesses during arrests of Indians. If there was a question concerning the legality of the arrest, they defended the Indian and demanded his release. In thirty-nine weeks of careful patrolling of the Indian areas of the Twin Cities, the arrest rate was reduced nearly to zero, indicating that there had been extensive police discrimination prior to the organization of the patrol (Brophy and Aberle, 1966: 46-47). Besides AIM, other groups have been instrumental in bringing about changes. For example, the Native American Rights Fund (NARF) successfully argued a class action suit for the Indian inmates in U.S. District Court against the director of the Nebraska Correctional Services Department. This suit was the forerunner of the Cheyenne River Swift Bird Project, which is a prototype of Indian-run correctional facilities in the United States. A part of this program included a survival school wherein Indians were taught a sense of self-worth and basic survival skills necessary to cope within both the Indian and the white worlds (French, 1980: 22).

Attitudes and Values

Native Americans value life—all living things. For them, the earth is Mother and the sky is Father. They believe in spirits. In all living things there is a spiritual essence. In fact, they believe that as human beings, we are both spiritual and physical. When our bodies die, our spirits continue to live. The awareness of spirit—both good and bad—has made Native Americans ward off the bad spirits by circle formation (i.e., sitting in circles, living in teepees). Because of this feeling of spiritual kinship with every living thing, the earth is sacred. Since the earth is living and is given as in trust from the "Great Spirit," how can it be sold to others? Hence, a conflict arises between the American-Anglo idea of personal property and the Indian idea of sharing and harmony.

Native Americans value their families. Children and the elderly both have significant roles to play. The extended family is cherished. The network of relationships is used to fulfill both emotional and physical needs. In fact, the supportive network may be used for child rearing and child management practices. Thus, child-rearing responsibilities may be delegated to specific relatives and/or older children. The child is accustomed to taking directions from and being cared for by numerous people. Parents believe in using a positive approach to child rearing. They give positive rewards; they do not use physical punishment, but rather lavish love and care on children.

Compared to Anglo-American standards, these child rearing practices are at times incorrectly interpreted as permissive or neglectful. The most dramatic example of such a problem is the tremendously disproportionate removal of Native American Indian children from their homes (Slaughter, 1976; Unger, 1977).

The traditional Indian culture places emphasis upon feelings. Like blacks, a majority of Indian students do not learn well from traditional classroom approaches (such as lecturing and matter-of-fact direction). Indians are used to stories and fables, which they are allowed to search and interpret for themselves. In a more affective model of teaching, children continue their search for knowledge and development of self, which brings positive self-esteem and a development of responsibility for their own success.

For the Indian, disease may be seen as a result of supernatural manifestations or the result of incorrect living. Thus, patients have great faith in medicine men or women. Sometimes their power in healing carries a psychological or spiritual dimension. Sometimes these healers are more knowledgeable about herbs and natural ways of helping the body heal itself. Treatment usually involves other family members, relatives, neighbors, and friends, who serve as a support for the patient. Although much of the literature has been developed for people in health-giving agencies, there are some important parallels for police (Everett, 1979: 2).

The Indian culture values the clan, the tribe, the extended family. Thus, attitudes of working together, of cooperation, and of giving mutual support or aid are fostered. As strange as it may seem, the Indian becomes both a member of a tribe and a proud individual (Steiner, 1968: 139-140). This spirit of both rugged individualism and emphasis on self-determination and noninterference is incompatible with coercive styles of intervention. Traditional Indian societies were usually organized through voluntary cooperation. Force or coercion was not generally employed. This has two implications: First, when the agent in the criminal justice system or would-be service provider is directive, coercive, or intrusive, the Native American may not say anything to the agent. Rather, the Indian client, not wanting to interfere with the Anglo's freedom to act as he or she sees fit, chooses to avoid conflict by avoiding the agent. Second, some Indians, when so isolated from others, especially in a small jail cell that does not provide a sense of communication with the world of nature, kill themselves. Thus, it is important, when securing the environment of a Native American, that one does not contribute to his or her death through lack of cultural awareness.

Indians value life such that everyone in the kinship family is responsible for the life and death of everyone else. The more traditional Indian even cherished the trees. He never cut down a living tree, for he believed it had a heart, like a human being. If all is equally alive, then all should be shared. Nature was considered beautiful. Indians were encouraged to walk in beauty, think beautiful thoughts, have beautiful images. The Navaho, in parting, will say, "Go in beauty." Those simple words expose the harmony of man with his spiritual and physical world in a circle that invites other people of peace.

Vested Interest Groups

To press their demands upon the larger society, Indians have increasingly organized themselves. The National Congress of American Indians, the National Indian Youth Council, and the American Indian Movement are associations which are tribally inclusive (Hraba, 1979: 235).

The Bureau of Indian Affairs (BIA) has an inconsistent reputation at best among the tribes. This is due largely to the past, when the Anglos operated the agency as part of the U.S. Department of the Interior. More recently, more Native Americans have taken leadership positions with the agency. Thus, the BIA has had an uneven history in regard to the welfare of the American Indian.

The goal of the Indian Health Services (IHS) is to offer comprehensive health services to Indian people. Health services may include water, sewer, and solid waste systems. For example, in 1979, the Papago Tribal Utility Authority worked with IHS and some Arizona consultants to develop standards to assess the conditions and identify the improvements in the various villages owned by the Papago tribe (Kundson, 1979). In one particular case, an older couple was given a toilet and inside plumbing. Two weeks later, the woman called and said, "Come get it now. It's full." The people who were installing the technology had forgotten to show her how to flush it. This is an example of differences in life experience, not necessarily intelligence or motivation.

Information about the BIA and IHS resources in a particular community can be obtained through the regional office of the BIA area in which the community is located. Since nearly half of all Indians live in the urban-suburban areas of the nation, almost every city of any size has an Indian center. These centers serve for powwows (dances), craft activities, and basketball and other sports activities. In addition, some of the larger centers, through federal grants, have been able to provide social services treatment for alcoholism, child and baby clinics, Boy Scout troops, and so on.

Spanish-Speaking Americans

Spanish-speaking Americans are not a racial group per se. Spanish-speaking Americans include such ethnic groups as Mexican Americans, Puerto Ricans, and Cubans. Each of these ethnic groups is different, even though they speak a similar language. Mexican Americans, for example, are often called "Chicanos," while the term "Hispanic" is often used to refer to Puerto Ricans, Cubans, and others of Latin American descent.

The matter of an appropriate name for this ethnic group is very problematic and controversial. Each term of group identification that has been adopted by one segment of the population has been considered offensive or inaccurate by another group or segment. Since the members of this population vary so widely in their specific histories, present geographic locations, and social characteristics, it is no wonder that various terms are used and applied. The term "Chicano," for example, is frequently used by younger members who favor cultural pluralism. The term "Mexican American" is usually preferred by older group members who favor assimilation or Anglo conformity in certain parts of their lives. In addition to the terms "Chicano" and "Mexican American," the terms "Latin American," "Spanish American," "Hispano," "Spanish surname," "La Raza," and "Mexicans" have been used during specific times for specific reasons. In this chapter, "Chicano" or "Mexican American" will be used to refer to those who trace their ancestry to Mexico either before or after the Spanish conquest. "Hispanic" will be used to refer to Puerto Ricans, Cubans, and others of Latin American descent.

In 1980, the Census Bureau for the first time used pointed questions to get statistics on the number of Mexicans, Puerto Ricans, Cubans, and other Spanish-speaking persons living in the United States. According to the 1980 census, the Spanish-speaking population of the United States resides mostly in the five Southwestern states. In addition, six states outside the Southwest—Illinois, Michigan, Washington, Florida, Indiana, and Ohio—had more than 50,000 persons of Mexican origin. Puerto Ricans are concentrated in New York, New Jersey, and Illinois. Cubans are located in such states as Florida, New Jersey, New York, California, Illinois, and Texas (in rank order).

From the 1980 census, blacks comprised 12 percent of the population and were ranked as the second largest racial or ethnic group in the country. However, many demographers believe that by the year 1990 or 2000, Spanish-speaking people will constitute the largest minority group in the United States (Pachon and Moore, 1981: 454). Their growth in numbers will be due largely to continued immigration and large family size (Pachon and Moore, 1981: 115). In addition, their median age is younger. For example, the median age is 31.3 years for whites, 24.9 for blacks, and 23.2 for Spanish-speaking people. All of these elements—larger family size, continued immigration, and younger median age—combine to assure a rapid growth in population. No doubt, this result will have tremendous social and economic consequences, including ramifications for the criminal justice system.

History

Strange as it may seem, some of these Hispanic people are citizens of the United States. Puerto Ricans, for example, are citizens of the United States and have been since 1917. As such, their movement to and from the mainland is unrestricted—much like movement between states on the mainland. When economic conditions become poor on their mainland, Puerto Ricans come to the United States for work.

Cubans, on the other hand, are not citizens of the United States. Their existence in this country is due to political problems in their country in more recent years. When Cuban exiles were first arriving in the United States, the government undertook an extensive resettlement program to scatter these people throughout cities other than Miami. Alas, besides the high concentration in New York City and New Jersey, many returned to Miami, where they have been a major influence in transforming it into a new and active Spanish-speaking center of international commerce. Relatively few of these exiled Cubans received public assistance, and their delinquency rates are low. These Cuban exiles are not, of course, those of more recent times, who are considered the criminals of their own society who are seeking refuge as boat people.

The Mexican Americans—the Chicanos—have a more extensive history in our country than do the Puerto Ricans or Cubans. The Southwestern states were settled by people of Spanish-Mexican-Indian ancestry long before they were settled by Anglo-Americans. Long before Mexico achieved independence in 1821, the Spaniards' policy of assimilation made the culture and population of Mexico an "Indianized" culture and population. That is not to say that the melting-pot process of assimilation was not without conflict. Indeed, there were hostile relations between the natives in Mexico and their Spanish conquerors. Nevertheless, the Christianizing and economic inclusion of the Indians created a new culture— the Hispano-Indian society of Mexico.

The Louisiana Purchase of 1803, whereby the United States bought a vast tract of land from France, did little to define the boundaries between that purchased land and the country of Mexico. Thus, there was an almost constant state of tension along the frontier—from a point west of New Orleans, through Texas to the Rocky Mountains, north along the Rockies and west to the Pacific. Much to the chagrin of Mexico, many Americans believed that Texas had been included in that purchase. Other Americans believed in the idea of a manifest destiny, which said that our country should span the continent—from sea to shining sea. Thus, the frontier should be extended to the Pacific, by force if necessary.

Struggles, wars, and battles led to the 1848 Treaty of Guadalupe Hidalgo. Mexico ceded to the United States more than one-half of her territory, with the Rio Grande establishing the boundary between the two countries. Except for Native Americans, Chicanos have been the only American ethnic minority to enter the society through conquest of their homelands. In other words, one day they were Mexican citizens; the next day, due to the treaty, the places where they lived were no longer in Mexico. At that point, Mexicans had either to leave their homes and move south of the newly established border or to declare themselves Mexican nationals within the United States and thereby acquire the rights of citizens of the United States.

The treaty of Guadalupe Hidalgo did not end the physical violence between the Anglos and Chicanos within the borderlands. Although there exists no accurate tabulation of the violent interethnic encounters that have taken place between individuals and groups, it has been reported that the number of Chicanos killed in the Southwest during the years 1850-1930 was greater than the number of lynchings of black Americans during that same period (Moquin and Van Dorect, 1971: 253). In Moore's (1976: 36) opinion, "No other part of the United States saw such prolonged intergroup violence as did the Border States from 1848 to 1925" [McLemore, 1980: 213].

Unfortunately, there are examples of discrimination even today. Besides Chicanos being part Mexican or Spanish, they are also part Indian. In 1979, a study done by the U.S. Department of Housing and Urban Development revealed that dark-skinned Mexican Americans experienced discrimination in housing more so than black Americans or light-skinned Mexican Americans (Hakken, 1979). In 1980, approximately 100,000 children were kept out of the Texas public school system by a law (later declared discriminatory by the Supreme Court) which stated that children of undocumented workers were debarred from public education unless they paid tuition (Pachon and Moore, 1981: 122). Some economists fear that Chicanos, in particular, and Hispanics, in general, are becoming a permanent underclass in this country due to the lack of economic opportunity, which in turn affects income, poverty, education, and health (Pachon and Moore, 1981: 118).

Today, throughout the borderlands between Mexico and the United States, Chicanos retain a strong, distinctive culture. Spanish has continued to be the primary spoken language. In addition, in the urban areas, Mexican Americans settle in neighborhoods or barrios where Spanish is spoken. In Los Angeles, for example, Chicanos "constitute the third largest urban concentration of people of Mexican descent outside of Mexico City and Guadalajara" (Pachon and Moore, 1981: 116).

It is well to remember that many of these suburban barrios are not the outgrowth of central-city expansion. Rather, these barrios are the result of the labor camps established at the beginning of this century for Mexican laborers and their families who worked in agriculture or on railroads. The work gangs included all family members, who lived in temporary and frequently unsanitary housing.

When the agricultural sector of the American economy is high, so is the demand for Mexican labor. When the economy is low, as it was in the 1920s, the United States discontinues the practice of issuing permanent visas at the border stations. In the 1920s, those who wished to leave Mexico and work in America were required to file an application at the U.S. consulate. As a result of fear that these immigrants would become public charges, the applicants were required to show that an American citizen would support them if necessary. Needless to say, the increased cost and inconvenience connected with legal entry into the United States created the problem we still have today—illegal immigrants, the so-called wetbacks (McLemore, 1981: 221).

Another historical condition that merits attention is the Mexican juvenile gang. Chicano gangs, like all other juvenile gangs, vary in their size, chief interest, age composition, and so on. Many of the gangs in the 1930s and early 1940s were probably more street-corner clubs than actual violence-producing groups. No doubt, as youth, their talk was big.

In 1950, for example, some 66 percent of Chicanos lived in urban areas. In 1970, more than 85 percent were urban dwellers (Mclemore, 1981: 240). Combine urban residency with more youthful populations of this ethnic group, and one is bound to produce spontaneous play activity groups, if not gang activity per se.

Like blacks and other ethnic groups before them, Chicano youths disproportionately served in the armed forces during World War II. The valor of these fighting persons earned the respect and admiration of their comrades. The old disloyal, undisciplined *pachucos* image gave way to one of a comrade accepted on equal terms. Accordingly, the veterans expected civilian life after the war to be far better than it had been before the war. Unfortunately, it was not. The bitter disappointment led in the 1960s to the awakening of the Chicanos and the present-day organized political and protest activities in all of the main sectors of American life.

Special Concerns

As with any ethnic group facing discrimination, there are many special concerns. For pragmatic reasons, however, this discussion will focus upon these four: (1) color, (2) religion, (3) gangs, and (4) language.

Color. Hispanic people—from various parts of the Caribbean and Central and South America—vary in skin coloring. Hispanic persons may be Caucasoid, Indio, Negroid, or a mixture of any of these. Cubans are mostly Caucasoid, although many of the recent refugees are Negroid. A black Puerto Rican is called Puerto Rican among his people, while an American black is called *moreno*. "Hostility and fear often mark the relations of Puerto Ricans and American Blacks" (Fitzpatrick and Parker, 1981). This hostility and fear is brought into the criminal justice system, where persons of all ethnic groups, especially minorities, are housed in lock-ups, jails, prisons, and the like.

Religion. Religious beliefs and practices can cause people to view their world differently. Most Chicanos and Hispanics have been baptized Catholic. For the law-abiding Hispanic, religion serves to routinize his or her lifestyle. It is among the poorest population in Cuba, with their folk religion called Santeria, that there are implications for law enforcement officers. Santeria as is frequently practiced is a mixture of spiritualism, African influences, and Catholic rites that involves elements of water, blood, fire, and smoke. Puerto Rican and Cuban neighborhoods are dotted with botanicas—small shops where charms, potions, herbs, candles, and religious paraphernalia, largely related to spiritism and animals, may be purchased. Chickens and doves are only some of the lesser animals used in the animal sacrifice rituals. Officials in Dade County, Florida, for example, have been perplexed by the increase in animal sacrifices, the improper disposal of the remains, and the public outcry. It becomes a difficult problem to control.

Gangs. Gangs are not merely a historical fact; they are a modern-day reality. According to the Chicago *Tribune* of September 7, 1977, "Latin street gang rivalry burst into violence over the weekend with one person shot to death and 12 others wounded in 48 hours" (Chicago Tribune, 1977).

East Los Angeles has also had a problem with gangs. Some local officials estimate that there are as many as 250 gangs in Los Angeles County, with members estimated at 22,500, ranging in age from thirteen to forty. Most members are Chicanos. In 1979, gang violence killed 300 people. Thus, with the help of federal funds, an unusual effort has been established: the Gang Violence Reduction Project. In essence, as Bernstein (1980: 46) reports, it hired and supervised fourteen hard-core gang leaders to: (1) keep communications open among project gangs; (2) settle disputes; (3) help fellow gang members find jobs, keep court dates, get drivers' licenses, return to school, and enroll in drug and alcohol rehabilitation programs; and (4) plan fun activities with members of different gangs that are not likely to erupt in violence (picnics, bowling tournaments, and the like).

Critics of the program resent the idea of paying gang members. Others, including local law enforcement agencies, have used another approach to gang violence: vigorous law enforcement that results in jail terms for gang members. To this end, the sheriff's department runs two programs: Operation Safe Street, a Law Enforcement and Assistance Administration (LEAA) project "which is directed solely against gang members, and a locally funded Gang Suppression Unit" (Bernstein, 1980: 47).

In terms of gangs, a word must be said about the Puerto Rican gangs epitomized in the famous musical *West Side Story*. "Ricans," "Nuyoricans," and "Neo-Ricans" are second-generation Puerto Ricans who have grown up in the ghettos of New York and other cities. As a result, Ricans have adopted the language of the streets and are more aggressive. During the 1960s, some of those youth joined groups such as the Young Lords, Ghetto Brothers, or Savage Skills. Some fell into drugs and delinquency; others moved toward community action and leadership (Fitzpatrick and Parker, 1981: 108).

Puerto Rican and Cuban terrorist groups, such as Alpha 66 and Omega 7, are, perhaps, the biggest problem facing law enforcement personnel today. Since our democratic society permits any group to grow, these terrorist groups will continue to be a challenge.

Language. The last special concern to be discussed is language. This is not to say that speaking Spanish is bad or wrong. Rather, it is to say that when persons who speak only Spanish come into contact with police and court personnel, their language may be a barrier. The language barrier, for example, is most difficult for an arresting officer. Without good communication, it is possible to apprehend the victim instead of the offender. In addition, Puerto Ricans in particular, like Greeks and Italians, use their hands to express themselves. Some situations become volatile because the officer at the scene of the crime is met by a large man who loudly speaks a foreign language, moves his hands up and down, and comes closer to the officer.

To avoid these unfortunate situations, some police departments hire more Spanish-speaking officers. Other departments have developed Spanish courses modeled after those of the United States Border Patrol and the Church of Jesus Christ of the Latter-Day Saints (Mormons). Officers are immersed in Spanish language and Hispanic culture (Tatum, 1978: 44-45). In addition, courts have had to utilize bilingual interpreters to assist Spanish-speaking citizens at key points in their defense.

In the previous discussion, four major special concerns were addressed: (1) color, (2) religion, (3) gangs, and (4) language. That discussion was to enlighten Anglo-Americans as to the special needs of Spanish-speaking persons. The discussion was not meant to be inclusive of all the concerns facing this particular group. Obviously, there are other concerns, which will vary from region to region in the United States.

Attitudes and Values

In this section, the goal is to acquaint the reader with some of the attitudes and values of Spanish-speaking persons. As with the sections on other specific ethnic groups, the attitudes and values herein expressed are those that have generally been identified as important to this particular group.

Mexican Americans think of themselves as citizens of the United States and as members of La Raza (the race). "La Raza" is a term that refers to a cultural and spiritual bond which unites them. It is the spiritual aspect that is most important, for it gives the Spanish-speaking person a worldview such that his or her spirit is divine and infinite.

The family is also very important. Children and the elderly both have important roles in the extended family. The mother, daughter, and sister relationships are especially close. The culture demands that a daughter be more tightly supervised during puberty in order to protect her purity. Thus, she is trained by her female guardians for the role in the home. The teenage boy, on the other hand, learns to be a man by being outside the home with male friends. Sexual promiscuity on the part of the wife is a heinous crime because her purity is so fragile. Because of this double standard or stereotype, women who have been raped by other men in the community need special assistance. To address this problem of rape and the role of women, the Queen's Bench Foundation, an organization of women lawyers and judges in San Francisco, provides a half-hour videotape in Spanish as part of its educational program. The videotape is written, directed, and enacted by Latins (Brodyaga et al., 1975: 130).

The spirit of "compadraggo" (social ties between parents and godparents) is also a part of the Mexican heritage. The Catholicism of godparents reinforces the sense of personal responsibility to help other people as part of the brotherhood. As for American Indians, the sense of family and extended family ties is extremely important. Felix J. Chaves (1976: 30), a probation officer in Los Angeles County, says that "the probation officer may in effect be counseling the whole extended family."

Because of this traditionally intense pride in the family name, there is resentment towards anglicizing a name. In addition, in Mexican culture, a formal address indicates respect for the dignity of the other person. Thus, Mexican persons expect to be addressed as Mr., Mrs., or Miss. By learning to pronounce the Spanish-speaking person's name, the agent in the criminal justice system will help establish the necessary respect required for the desired rapport.

Lastly, Spanish-speaking persons place a high value on close, warm personal relationships. Because of this attitude, the cool, crisp, efficient, and impersonal way in which persons are handled by agencies is viewed as frightening rather than professional. Likewise, this culture is more tolerant of dependency and less concerned with initiative and self-determination. Thus, agents may have to do more with these individuals in a friendly manner so that they do not feel that they are being rejected or being given grudging assistance. (For more special attention to Hispanics, see Carter, 1983.)

Vested Interest Groups

Mexican Americans have a long history of groups representing their concerns and causes. The League of United Latin American Citizens (LULAC) was begun in the 1920s in Texas and still is operating today. The GI Forum was established in the 1940s and the Mexican American Political Association (MAPA) in the 1950s. Other public interest groups include the Mexican American Legal Defense and Education Fund (MALDEF) and the National Council of La Raza. The Congressional

Hispanic Caucus and the National Association of Latino Elected and Appointed Officials (NALEAO) are examples of organizations intent upon unifying Hispanic groups and articulating their concerns (Pachon and Moore 1981: 122-123).

Grass-roots organizations have also been important. Among Puerto Ricans, Aspira tries to promote educational opportunities and excellence both in New York City and on the national level. The Puerto Rican Family Institute is a citywide agency in New York City and in Puerto Rico, in the field of family service. The Puerto Rican Legal Defense and Education Fund has a notable record in class action suits in representing the Puerto Rican community on the local and national levels. The Puerto Rican Forum is an organization that serves as an advocate in the business and community arenas.

SER—Jobs for Progress—is a nonprofit corporation composed of representatives of major Hispanic organizations. Funded by the U.S. Department of Labor, SER aims to provide employment opportunities for disadvantaged Spanish-speaking and Hispanic-surnamed Americans. Each local program is organized according to local conditions and needs. Thus, it is responsible for the recruitment and selection of job trainees, counseling, prejob orientation and vocational preparation, basic education, employer relations and follow-up services to trainees after training and job placement (Yakes and Akey, 1980: 75).

There are many more organizations, both local and national, that might be consulted for more information. In particular, the National Puerto Rican Coalition has been established in Washington, D.C. That organization can be consulted for more information on Puerto Ricans. The National Council of La Raza, 1725 Eye Street, N.W., Washington, D.C., has also been instrumental in assisting Hispanic organizations to develop community public relations programs in areas such as crime prevention (Lockard et al., 1978: 22).

Asian Americans

In different localities throughout the United States, agents in the criminal justice system may experience other minority groups not previously discussed. Asian Americans might be such a group. The term "Asian American" covers more than twenty nationalities representing such countries as China, Japan, Guam, Samoa, Vietnam, and Cambodia. Each group has its own identity and culture.

The recent wars and political unrest in Indochina have caused people from Laos, Vietnam, and Cambodia to come to the United States as refugees. These Asian Americans, also known as "boat people," escaped their countries and lived in deplorable conditions on boats. Many documented reports tell of the disease and death aboard the boats and the reluctance of other countries to accept these people because of filled quotas. Some refugees were therefore put back to sea to look for refuge elsewhere.

The refugees who do come to the United States tend to be sponsored by private and government agencies. Because of this individual attention, they quickly become self-supporting, and within five years their employment rate is the same as the average for all Americans. In some localities, unfortunately, they have not been treated well. The local antagonism inflamed by such groups as the Ku Klux Klan (KKK) has resulted in their boats being set afire and their families being forced to move (Auden, 1981: 381).

Remembering the corruption of South Vietnam's courts and police, the Vietnamese in America have little faith and/or trust in our law enforcement agents. They become easy victims for intimidation and the collection of protection money. Because of their distrust, Vietnamese witnesses are unwilling to cooperate with investigators even in the most brutal cases. They, like some Americans, fear that they will incur retaliation if they testify against a specific person.

Being misinformed about the criminal justice system, the Vietnamese in America become prey to criminals within their own ethnic group. These ethnic gangs—some with postmilitary training and experience—become a real challenge for law enforcement. Breaking the code of silence and the language barrier places an especially heavy burden on law enforcement officials in Central and Southern California.

The Handicapped

Since law enforcement officers are trained to be suspicious—to look for the unusual—handicapped individuals need to understand that their condition might arouse curiosity or be mislabeled by agents in the criminal justice system. On the other hand, agents must be alerted to the possibility that in the course of performing their duties, they may encounter physically handicapped individuals. Thus, training to handle encounters with physically and mentally handicapped individuals is in order.

Two such groups committed to making officers more aware of the handicapped are the Iowa Law Enforcement Academy and the Des Moines Police Academy (Peebles, 1980: 44-45). Both use lecturing psychologists to give insights into handling encounters between officers and handicapped individuals. Besides their approach, agencies could use a panel presentation in which both handicapped and nonhandicapped individuals are participants. Presentations could deal with possible consequences of misunderstandings and identifications. Local chapters of the United Cerebral Palsy Fund or Muscular Dystrophy Association are good places to contact speakers and/or panel candidates.

Agents in the criminal justice system should have the opportunity to interact informally with handicapped individuals. Once an officer realizes that there are both law-abiding handicapped citizens and non-law-abiding handicapped citizens, it will be easier for the agent to deal realistically with the situation. Agents who are unaware of the nature of handicapped individuals often have unrealistic expectations. For example, some agents talk louder to blind people, as if the blindness also causes them to be hard of hearing or deaf. Handicapped persons need not lose their freedom because of fear of crime and victimization. Two veteran police officers—one a paraplegic due to an on-duty motorcycle accident as a patrolman for the Memphis, Tennessee, Police Department—have developed a videotape on wheelchair self-defense to be used to help handicapped people survive.[3]

Another group of handicapped persons that gives agents in the criminal justice system special problems is the deaf. According to the 1970 census, there were more than 13 million Americans with hearing impairments. Of that number, at that time, about 5 million persons had slight hearing impairments, 6 million suffered from significant hearing loss, and 2 million persons were completely deaf. Most of these people work, shop, drive cars, and function in nearly every walk of life. The challenge arises when a deaf person is at the scene of an auto accident (either as the victim or a witness), at a traffic stop, or in a burning building. Understanding that a person who seemingly ignores an order to move on or to step back at a fire scene cannot hear commands because he or she is deaf is the first step in developing a sensitivity to this problem.

Contrary to popular belief, most deaf persons cannot lip-read. In fact, 60 percent of English words look exactly like some other word on the lips. Thus, Ameslan (American Sign Language) is the sign language most often used ("The Deaf and the Police," 1976). There is still no universally agreed-upon set of hand signals, however.

If a deaf person needs to be arrested, then Miranda warnings have to be issued. To achieve this, an officer may show the warnings in print. Yet many deaf persons are undereducated. Thus, an interpreter may be needed. Names of competent interpreters can be obtained from the Registry of Interpreters for the Deaf, Inc., a national certifying organization located at Gallaudet College, P.O. Box 1339, Washington, D.C., 20013.

To assist with callers to police stations who are deaf, some police departments have purchased or rented a special telecommunications device referred to as a TTY. A TTY consists of a receiver and a typewriter keyboard, which are used to transmit and receive written communication using the telephone. If the cost is prohibitive for small departments, then service organizations such as the Lions or Rotary can be asked to lend support (Miller, 1980: 69).

In conclusion, handicapped individuals pose special problems for agents in the criminal justice system, from arrest through conviction to treatment (Tidyman, 1974). Yet people in the community who suffer from these conditions are often very willing to teach others. Organizations that assist handicapped persons should be contacted for their expertise. The sharing of information between agencies will go a long way toward building better community and public relations.

SUMMARY

In this chapter, the discussion has centered on three major ethnic groups: blacks, American Indians, and Spanish-speaking Americans. Each group has its own particular history. Yet there have been several major themes throughout the discussion. First, all of these groups have experienced tremendous discrimination. Whereas they might not now be experiencing the death and destruction of former years, they are, nonetheless, experiencing discrimination in more subtle terms. Many of these minorities did not come to America as invaders. It is no wonder some groups protest the evil that lingers around them and/or their children. Credit must be given to many of them for their courage.

Second, all of these groups value strong extended families, the tendency toward mutual aid, the brother/sisterhood of humankind, and warm interpersonal relationships.

Many of these groups share the same complaints against agents in the criminal justice system. Many believe the police have a tendency to be harsher with the minority person than with the majority offender. Others are upset by the indifference shown when one ethnic person commits a crime against another ethnic person. Stereotypes and lack of awareness on the part of agents in the criminal justice system make it hard to identify the criminal in the midst of the minority population. Others complain about the use of excessive force and the unnecessary field interrogation, which they perceive to be in violation of their constitutional rights. The landmark Supreme Court cases dealing with the police interrogation of suspects, Escobedo v. Illinois and Miranda v. Arizona, certainly support their perception. Some minorities complain that there is less rigorous law enforcement in their areas. They feel that the police have decided that illegal activities such as drug addiction, prostitution, and street violence are appropriate in their neighborhoods. Others complain that they are too often the victims and do not know how to stop the criminal. Still others complain about the courts, the wide disparity in sentences, the antiquated corrections facilities, the inequities imposed by the system on the poor and the total lack of effective channels for the redress of complaints against the conduct of police, judges, and correctional personnel.

It would stand to reason that if some of these complaints are to be resolved, then agents need to be able to differentiate between law-abiding ghetto residents and ghetto criminals. When officers are more informed and more comfortable with their feelings, they are less likely to violate the rights of decent citizens. One's own fears and stereotypes are held in abeyance.

In conclusion, as long as countries throughout the world experience wars, rumors of wars, and political upheavals, then this country will always experience new people. The United States is one of the few countries in the world that is stable enough and democratic enough to permit others the chance to exercise their own free will. Thus, this country will also experience ethnic groups. Our challenge will be to understand enough about new groups' cultures that they feel valued while we teach them the coping skills necessary to live in this country.

DISCUSSION QUESTIONS

(1) Our society often espouses the "melting pot" theory. What happens to people when they are not permitted their differences? What are the advantages and disadvantages of having everyone on a specific level?

(2) Recall a scene before you were twelve years old when you had your first experience with a person of a different race or ethnic background.

What do you remember? What happened? What were your feelings? What messages did that give you that carry with you even today? What have you learned from others as to how to feel, think, or behave in response to people whose color is different from yours?

(3) Since we live in a multicultural, multilingual, and pluralistic society, what could people do to be more culturally aware and sensitive to other people?

(4) Is the concern by minority groups over police brutality justified? Is it possible for white officers to find trust and acceptance in a minority community? Explain.

NOTES

1. For the scheme presented in this section, I am indebted to Joseph Hraba, *American Ethnicity* (1979), who uses this scheme throughout his book.

2. Although anthropologists and sociologists since the 1920s have argued that there are no pure racial groups, today there are groups that believe they are racially different. To satisfy that concern, this text will use the phrase "ethnic and racial."

3. Contact Steve Reddish, Para Media Productions, 2080 Sharon Lane, Memphis, Tennessee 38127.

PART IV

Partnerships

6

PARTNERSHIP AND MANAGEMENT OF CITIZEN PARTICIPATION

In this chapter, attention is given to partnerships—citizens and police working together. As mentioned in Chapter 1, historically speaking, communities have generally felt a sense of responsibility for their problems, even though they may not always have developed a program to deal with them. Borrowing from the English tithing system, the early American colonists continued an active involvement in their communities. The early policing functions were fulfilled by citizens. In later years, appointed or elected officials fulfilled all or most of the enforcement duties. Yet, even at that time, citizens as noncommissioned officers were deputized for emergencies, as in the western posse or vigilante groups.

In short, the present volunteer movement in police, courts, and corrections is far from new. Our ancestors have always been concerned with questions of law and order. Although sometimes the only method they seemed to employ to alleviate the community problem was banishment or capital punishment, the fact remains that people felt concern. For example, concern for the futility of the old ways motivated the Quakers in Philadelphia in 1773 to develop their community-based corrections program. Today, we call their endeavors the Walnut Street Jail and the beginning of the American prison system. In this community-based operation, the spirit of firmness and friendliness was used to aid the reformation of the offender as he or she engaged in hard work and silence, contemplating his or her behavior to seek penitence (Barnes and Teeters, 1959: 336).

Besides their concern for their problems, the early, good-hearted, religiously inspired community persons volunteered their services and visited offenders. As early as 1823 in Philadelphia, an organization known as the Society of Women Friends made it their objective to visit women in the segregated quarters in jails and workhouses (Barnes and Teeters, 1959: 408). Another example is John Augustus, who, in 1841, volunteered his service to the court in Boston, Massachusetts, to help with misdemeanants. Often called the father of volunteerism, in his eighteen years of service to the court before his death, John Augustus had "bailed on probation some 2,000 persons including women, children and persons charged with a wide variety of offenses" (United Nations, 1976: 89-90).

In more recent years, starting in the 1950s and 1960s, citizen participation again became important. Although the first image-building community relations program was installed in St. Louis, Missouri, in the 1950s, it took the social unrest of the 1960s for the need of citizen involvement to become paramount.

The 1960s especially challenged the assumptions of, and generated a national concern with, issues of race, poverty, violence, and international responsibilities. The "grass-roots approach" to alleviating poverty, such as community action councils, was only part of the increased public concern with and acceptance of citizen participation and community programs that would later seep into criminal justice programs as well.

Research concerning crime and delinquency, as early as the 1920s, has continued to show communities the role they can play in creating crime and, subsequently, what they might do to alleviate the problems. Sociologists in the 1960s showed how crime was linked more to social factors than to individual factors such as "free will" and "rationalism." Their emphasis upon social factors did not ignore psychological, physical, or other individual characteristics, but rather considered them as they occurred in a particular setting. "If the social milieu to a substantial degree causes criminal behavior, the social milieu itself must be attacked and changed" (National Advisory Commission on Criminal Justice Standards and Goals, 1976: 494). The War on Poverty became a concerted effort to fight the influences causing crime.

Thus, the maximum feasible participation concept operationalized in the poverty programs of the 1960s began to be utilized in the criminal justice system. Citizens were again being sought as policymakers, as reformers, and as deliverers of direct services. The partnership between citizens and public agencies was again developing.

PARTNERSHIP: POLICE AND CITIZENS

Today, often at the request of criminal justice officials, lay citizens function in task forces or study groups to advise the government in policy decisions. Recently, these advisory boards have included not only "leading citizens" but also representatives of minorities, ex-offenders, and other special community interest groups. Sometimes policymaking citizens will emerge through voluntary associations such as state citizen councils on crime and delinquency affiliated with the National Council on Crime and Delinquency, a nongovernmental agency.

Besides citizens acting in partnership with criminal justice agencies, some citizen groups have also emerged to act as reformers in response to specific societal situations. For example, after the prison riot in Attica, New York, in 1972, an informal group of persons created an organization to oppose correctional programs, and other correctional reform groups have developed out of religious and other social groups (Taft, 1979).

Feeling and assuming more responsibility for the problems they generate, communities either have developed new programs with new agencies or have used and coordinated existing community service agencies. Persons who can be instrumental in establishing these programs have been referred to as "gatekeepers." These individuals are not utilized as volunteers, but rather they are asked to use the power which adheres to their status in service of some community effort. These individuals become social persuaders, using their group memberships to mobilize resources.

The role citizens are asked to play most often is the one in which they help to deliver direct services. In 1959, Municipal Court Judge Keith J. Leenhouts of Royal Oak, Michigan, revived the volunteer movement. The judge, faced with neither presentence reports nor probation services, enlisted other concerned citizens to find some alternatives to the needs of the court. The group volunteered their services to the "probationers" of the court. When individuals needed the expertise of a professional, the volunteers sought out professionals who, at reduced costs, rendered their services or joined in the collaborative rehabilitation effort. The one-on-one approach of volunteers with probationers was so successful that Judge Leenhouts was instrumental in the establishment of volunteers in probation programs in more than 2000 locations. In 1972, the Volunteers in Probation (VIP), which had been formalized in 1969, became affiliated with the National Council on Crime and Delinquency (NCCD). Thus, it is known today as VIPNCCD.

Today, the use of volunteers in police, courts, and corrections—both inside and outside the institution—is massive. According to the estimates of the National Information Center on Volunteers, citizen volunteers outnumber professionals four or five to one (Scheier et al., 1972: iii). Because of this fact, there is substantial material to assist persons desiring to maximize the citizen's involvement, such as research information, organization and management aids, training guides, and audiovisual materials. The National Information Center on Volunteers in Courts (Boulder, Colorado), the National Council on Crime and Delinquency (Hackensack, New Jersey), and the Commission on Voluntary Service and Action (Washington, D.C.) are all organizations that can be consulted for this information.

To provide a better understanding of this partnership, the citizen's role will be discussed in terms of (1) citizen participation and (2) volunteers.

Citizen Participation Groups

There is a difference between citizen participation groups and programs that enlist volunteers. The major distinction is that citizen participation groups seek to take an active, decision-making or program implementation role, while volunteer groups usually participate actively in already established procedures and workings of the agency or department they serve. There are, of course, differences within each category as well as between categories of groups. Generally speaking, however, citizen participation groups consist of (1) public relations groups, (2) political pressure groups, (3) citizen review boards, (4) crime prevention programs, and (5) operational level intervention groups.

Public Relations Groups

Public relations groups usually involve the personnel of the agency as well as citizens who want to take an active part in educating the public about the police, the courts, or correctional organizations. As a public speakers bureau, these citizens pass on information to uninformed citizens.

Political Pressure Groups

Political pressure groups are known by a host of titles (including the Women's Bail Fund, the National Association for the Advancement of Colored People, the American Friends Service Committee, and prison projects named after specific states, such as the Alabama Prison Project). Citizen-observer teams with the police, the courts, and corrections attempt to mount independent political power to confront the forces in the criminal justice system. Usually, their appeals to public opinion create political pressure. With the police, special citizen patrols go to crime scenes to protect the rights of minority persons such as American Indians, Mexican Americans, and blacks. The effectiveness of these groups usually depends on the strength of the group and the vulnerability of the leaders involved.

STRANGER — DANGER!

TO DISCUSS AT SCHOOL AND HOME

How can I help Officer Friendly?

THE DUTIES OF OFFICER FRIENDLY

Here is your good friend Officer Friendly welcoming you back to school again. Night and day Officer Friendly protects you, keeps you safe, and helps you in many ways. Here is part of a long list of Officer Friendly's duties. Perhaps you will think of others.

1. Officer Friendly helps people to cross the street safely
2. Officer Friendly helps lost children to get home safely
3. Officer Friendly helps people who become sick on the street or have accidents

SOURCE: National Officer Friendly Program, The Sears-Roebuck Foundation. Reprinted by permission of The Sears-Roebuck Foundation.

NOTE: The Officer Friendly Program was initiated in Chicago in 1966. The Sears-Roebuck Foundation continues its efforts to establish better relationships between students, teachers, parents, and uniformed officers. Using an updated curriculum and teaching tools (as illustrated by the three pictures above, each representing an 8½-by-11-inch page from the complete set of 64 pages), the program seeks to promote crime resistance among children by stressing personal safety in the home, neighborhood, and street, and to increase children's awareness of the work of police officers and the wide array of services performed. The teaching tools are used in conjunction with uniformed officers who go to the classroom to enhance the teaching-learning experience. These materials are also an example of what companies and organizations in the community can do to sponsor, support, and cooperate with local law enforcement agencies and schools to help citizens, young and old, gain an understanding and respect for people who help build an orderly community.

Figure 6.1 Excerpts from the National Officer Friendly Program, sponsored by the Sears-Roebuck Foundation

Citizen Review Boards or Advisory Boards

Citizen review boards are probably the most controversial of all the citizen participation groups. The idea behind citizen review boards was to provide a bridge between the police departments and the communities they serve, so that citizens could complain about police conduct. Citizens who could be understanding of both sides were to be appointed to the board to review the matter. The citizen review board was an attempt at holding police officers accountable for their behavior and reducing conflict between citizenry and police by providing a legitimate channel for complaints and grievances. Unfortunately, experiments in Philadelphia, Pennsylvania; Rochester, New York; New York City, and a number of other cities showed that review boards were not very successful.

Philadelphia's Police Advisory Board (PAB), the first civilian review board in the country, had no investigation staff of its own. That meant that the board had to rely upon the police department's Community Relations Unit to investigate complaints. Needless to say, this strategy compromised the board's independence and the objectivity of the received reports. Upon completion of the investigation, the PAB would decide if a public hearing into a specific situation was warranted. Based upon that hearing, the PAB—which was strictly advisory and did not have any power—made recommendations to the police commissioner. The recommendations followed along the lines of reprimands, suspensions, dismissals, or commendations for the officers in question.

From 1958, when the PAB was created, until its end in 1967, the PAB recommended to the police commissioner discipline procedures for a police officer in only 6 percent of the cases. That means that most of the dispositions were the result not of public hearings but rather of informal hearings in which conciliation, an apology, or an explanation to the citizen took place. As the years went by, the PAB got fewer complaints filed from citizens and growing complaints about its operations from police officers (Robin, 1980: 85).

Litigation by police officers' organizations brought injunctions keeping the boards from functioning in Philadelphia and New York City. Moreover, other problems—limited budgets, limited powers, and limited staffing—emerged, so that citizen complaints could not be fully investigated. Police felt that the boards, instead of getting to the root of specific problems, singled out police for special blame. In addition, the adversarial nature of the proceedings did more to polarize the complainant, on the one side, and the accused police officer, on the other, than to develop a compromise.

Although citizen review boards in police agencies have not had an impressive history of successes or the endorsement of police officers, the lack of involvement of citizens in a reviewing or advisory capacity creates a void. In its place, a less satisfactory review is emerging: the internal review of complaints. The consensus seems to be that if police, court, or corrections personnel foul up, the criminal justice system would rather that their "own kind" handle the situation. Through a formal internal review process, action is supposed to be taken with regard to an officer's action. Yet, for the citizen, procedures used for filing complaints seem cumbersome and discouraging. The thought of a police officer being reviewed by an all-police personnel board leads citizens to wonder if complainants will get a fair, impartial hearing. For police officers, being charged and investigated by their "own kind" often means that they have fewer civil rights than the normal citizen—lacking notice of formal charges, representation of counsel, and the like (Krajick, 1980).

In specific areas of abuse, the lack of a meaningful review board or channels of communication concerning agents' behavior has only increased the number of lawsuits against police, correctional personnel, and agencies, and has served only to satisfy political, activist groups. The problem area that has received nationwide attention has been the sexual abuse of victims and/or offenders at the hands of criminal justice agents.

While there remains an absence of local redress for grievances, citizens are left to other external review mechanisms, such as the U.S. attorney's office, the state attorney general, or the district attorney. More and more, people are coming to the conclusion that some alternative needs to be developed which listens to citizens and supports administrators in holding agents accountable for their behavior. Even though earlier citizen review boards were problematic, present citizen advisory boards are doing commendable jobs in their areas. Perhaps the needs of the time will generate a newer, more equitable solution.

Crime Prevention Programs

Crime prevention programs are a more popular and less controversial form of citizen participation. With limited law enforcement responsibilities, these citizens seek to decrease criminal opportunities. Organized into groups such as block watchers, auxiliaries, telephone relays, and citizen patrols, these groups serve as the "eyes and ears" for the police, and they educate others in order to minimize their becoming victims of a crime.

To provide a better idea of the operationalization of this concept into resident patrols, the Rand Corporation in March 1976 published its findings from exploratory research in sixteen urban areas, which revealed more than 200 resident patrols that varied in their ratio of citizens. For example, some

> patrols involved situations in which residents themselves patrol or hire guards to patrol a residential area, maintaining some surveillance routine to the exclusion of other occupational activities. Some patrols cover neighborhood sections with members driving cars and maintaining contact through citizen band radios. Other patrols cover specific buildings or projects, with members stationed at a building entrance and monitoring passage by strangers into and out of the building [Yin et al., 1976: v].

As might be expected, some groups have worked independently of the police. Of course, they have selected citizens and trained participants themselves and have cooperated with the police. On the other hand, in some cities the police sponsor the program and ask for citizen participation on a volunteer basis to help maintain an integrated police-community approach to crime prevention. Examples of that approach come from Cottage Grove, Oregon, and St. Louis, Missouri. The crime prevention units of those police departments are routinely requested by the public to inspect their homes. Then, senior citizens, after being trained, go into those same houses to secure the dwelling. These volunteers are also sent to houses that have been broken into so as to make all the necessary repairs to make the house secure (Willis, 1976; D'Angelo, 1977).

To be sure, criminal activity is the result of three elements working together: (1) criminal desire, (2) criminal skill, and (3) opportunity. In order to break the cycle, it is important to stop one of these elements from contributing. In crime prevention, most attention is paid to the element of opportunity. Programs to reduce criminal opportunity might be surveillance and community reporting, such as Crime Watches, and teaching and counseling specific groups—bicycle security and safety for schoolchildren or sexual assault protection for college students. It may even mean having police specialists on urban planning boards so that criminal opportunity is denied due to the principles of environmental security, emphasizing target-hardening and defensible space.

Programs aimed at broadening the legitimate opportunity structure have usually concentrated on the area of employment, education, and recreation. For example, in recreation, most noted have been police athletic leagues (PALs). PAL programs are usually operated by local police departments to (1) prevent and reduce juvenile delinquency and

(2) promote better police-youth relationships in the community. The underlying principle of the program rests with channeling youths' overabundance of time and energy into socially acceptable outlets—supervised sports and skill-learning activities. The officer in these activities is afforded the opportunity to relate to the youth as a teacher, friend, and coach. In teaching how to play sports according to the rules, it is hoped that the program will instill in youth the principles of responsibility and sportsmanship. Once youths have experienced success on the athletic field, the hope is that they will begin to perceive themselves in a more positive manner and will sense their capabilities to achieve success through legitimate channels in their lives.

Of the more than 200 police athletic league programs currently in operation, the Albuquerque, New Mexico, Police Athletic League deserves special mention. Organized in 1973 by Albuquerque police officers, the program has developed to the point where it employs five full-time police officers and utilizes the services of more than 200 volunteers. The PAL program services approximately 6000 boys and girls in more than twenty-five activities, such as boxing, bicycling, wrestling, judo, tennis, football, softball, chess, backpacking, camping, and motocross racing. That PAL program, as in other cities across the nation, is dependent upon community support in the form of financial assistance and volunteers.

The athletic league of the police department in Salt Lake City, Utah, exhibits the differences in the structural alignment that can occur. In this case, the athletic and recreational program is a function of the Crime Prevention and Community Affairs Bureau. That bureau is then responsible for the so-called normal tasks of crime prevention activities, such as writing materials, planning and implementing conferences, and speaking to citizen groups. In addition, the crime prevention officers engage in the establishment of community organization and participation in crime prevention projects. To facilitate that effort of this bureau, the police department has created an advisory council and a businessmen's executive council. The advisory council consists of representatives from various minority groups, social agencies, and church organizations to advise the bureau, to consolidate efforts in the alleviation of crime and delinquency in the city and thereby decrease the amount of overlap in the functions and caseloads of present agencies. Most important, this advisory council helps to open various avenues of assistance to the bureau. The Businessmen's Executive Council has four major goals: (1) the establishment of a film library for department training and community services, (2) the appropriation and allocation of peace-officer training funds, (3) the creation of opportunities for improved youth employment, and (4) the betterment of recreational facilities for youth. Thus, in this organizational model, the community is invited into the police organization to help administer programs dealing with youth.

Operational Level Intervention Groups

Intervention groups usually consist of professional citizens who are asked, on either a paid or a gratis basis, to assist at a particular operational level. These groups usually consist of advisory boards, community profiling, and collaborative development for such things as a police policy manual.

Volunteers

Besides the five generally accepted types of citizen participation groups just discussed, there are various groups that are individually created in different settings. In this particular area, citizens volunteer to work within the agency. Some of the more well-known programs include police and sheriff reserves and the use of professional specialists. With this approach, the volunteer in the program or the entire program itself is viewed as complementing the agency's goals and offering assistance when needed, as opposed to attempting to change police, courts, or correctional policies.

Police-Sheriff Reserves, Auxiliary Patrols, and Community Service Officers

Reserve units, auxiliary patrols, and community service officers are usually composed of trained adult, community persons who volunteer their time to do limited police work (without remuneration). As trained persons, they can assist regular commissioned officers. They can assist, for example, in high-burglary areas by riding special details, looking for crimes, suspicious characters, and/or cars. They may be used in stakeouts or in directing traffic to and from large recreational events, such as football and baseball games. Although uniformed and wearing badges, these citizens, as reserve or auxiliary persons, are not armed and have no more law enforcement powers than do ordinary citizens. "Los Angeles has about 500 members (including 95 women) in its police reserve corps, with 400 others awaiting the required five-and-one-half-month training program; another 1,900 citizens are in the Los Angeles sheriffs' reserves" (Robin, 1980: 103). After taking a ten-week training program, 5400 persons work as police auxiliaries for New York City; 100 of those persons patrol Central Park on horseback in the evenings and on week-ends (Robin, 1980: 103n78). In San Diego, California, the "community service officer" came into being in March 1978 as part of a grant proposal for a program to solve staffing, recruitment, and budgetary problems (Shearer et al., 1977). The community service officer (CSO), like the reserve officer, carries no weapons and makes no arrests. Generally a youth between seventeen and twenty-one years of age, the CSO's attention is directed to police-community relations programs. CSOs are generally from minority groups and thus have a greater understanding of ghetto problems. Some of the tasks they are asked to do include working with juveniles to prevent delinquency, referring citizen complaints to appropriate agencies, and investigating minor thefts.

Sometimes called police service officers or police aides, CSOs are paraprofessionals who do the nonhazardous and less technical police duties at salaries below the level of police officers. This program also serves as a recruitment tool, because when these paraprofessionals are of the legal age for entrance into police work, many of them apply for open positions.

Programs such as the Explorers and the Police Cadets involve even younger persons and have the same basic purposes: (1) to serve as a recruitment tool, (2) to make a community relations effort, and (3) to provide a service group (Shearer et al., 1977). As an example of the contribution these young persons (between the ages of fourteen and twenty) can make in one particular city, the statistics during the year 1976 showed that they contributed more than 7000 hours to their communities through crime prevention and community service projects. This has been calculated to have yielded a savings of more than $60,000 in police salaries as well as an increase in the availability of line personnel and increased police services to the community (Shearer et al., 1977).

Professional Specialists

Professional services have been donated by many persons (such as psychologists, to analyze crime patterns, and owners and operators of aircraft, helicopters, boats, horses, and snowmobiles, for rescue missions). Ministers of religious organizations have a long history of involvement with criminal justice agencies. Involvement has included spiritual and personal counseling to persons in confinement and to those identified by the police as in need of consolation (such as persons involved in accidents, natural catastrophes, or the death of a loved one). Sometimes police chaplains have been used to defuse family disputes, to calm attempted suicide victims, and to counsel police officers with marital or alcohol problems.

As many people who work in human and social services are aware, many clients have multiple health, marriage, education, and job difficulties which demand concerted, organized efforts in order to break self-defeating behavior. As these professionals from other walks of life work with criminal justice agencies, they allow other nonpaid staff persons to be permitted into the agency to work as paraprofessionals.

Today, due to the acceptance of volunteers, it would be hard to find an agency that does not use volunteers to some degree. Moreover, it is amazing the number of organizations that encourage their employees to volunteer for community service. Most noted have been professional ballplayers. The National Football League has a charity fund, and the National Baseball Association, Professional Golf Association, and Professional Bowlers Association have all kinds of resources (speakers, films, demonstrations, and team players in off season), which are used by agents in the criminal justice system in programs for crime prevention with youth or as personal enrichment for the incarcerated.

PROS AND CONS

Utilization of citizens or unpaid staff poses both assets and liabilities. Some of the major pros and cons will be discussed to help one decide at which point and in which program the services of a citizen might be effective and efficient. (For a more lengthy discussion on the pros and cons of citizen involvement, see Matthews et al., 1969: 1-131.)

Pros

Citizens, especially those middle-class and upper-middle-class persons who structure some volunteer dimension into their lives, can be extremely useful on citizen advisory committees. They can help establish a convenient communication link with the so-called "Establishment" of any agency. In particular, they can help establish the credibility of the police with their publics. In this manner, then, they can help break down police isolation and occupational solidarity with the people the police serve.

Citizens are useful because they can give of their time in a more directed approach than can the paid staff, who usually have numerous other activities which require their attention. As seen with community service officers, police officers can direct their attention to more serious calls while others work in operation identification, bicycle safety, and house identification (the stenciling of house numbers on street curbs, which enables police and fire officials to identify homes more easily).

Citizens also provide additional sources of information and viewpoints. Heard by the agency in a one-on-one situation, citizens may exercise more progressive changes than angry, demanding groups who are tired of listening and want change only according to their definition.

As trained employees, citizens also create a more educated group of persons in our society who are more sensitized to the criminal justice system and its problems. Not only do they become better citizens; they also become sympathetic supporters.

Finally, citizens as paraprofessionals can be equated with a tremendous reservoir of energy extremely useful for emergencies. They can alleviate critical shortages of paid professional personnel while serving as a recruitment pool for future positions.

Cons

The incorporation of volunteers into agencies involved in the criminal justice system can produce a phenomenon called "more trouble than they are worth." The reasons are vast and varied. The following list will provide an idea of the troubles without exhausting the possible problematic situations:

(1) People who are "joiners" or have time and/or money often lack sensitivity to minorities. Thus, they may perpetuate a bias instead of decreasing interclass hostilities and misunderstandings.
(2) Citizen advisory committees lack direct policy-setting responsibilities.
(3) Some citizens desire profit and gain for themselves. Thus, they develop programs that are mere window dressing, so as not to change the status quo.
(4) Some citizens lack professional qualifications and training (Horejsi, 1973).
(5) Since volunteers receive no pay, they cannot be docked or penalized for early withdrawal from the volunteer program.
(6) Citizens lack awareness of the criminal justice system in general and specific agencies in particular.
(7) Because of the use of volunteers and/or citizen participation, some communities and politicians fail to take responsibility for solving the larger social problem and/or refuse to hire adequate numbers of personnel or pay better wages.

To conclude this section, it is worth emphasizing that there is little clear and convincing evidence for the effectiveness of citizen participation and volunteer programs. For example, arson squads, child abuse task forces, and sexual assault task forces are only a few of the many areas of concern that have developed an integrated, interdependent, open social system between and among social service agencies, hospitals, and other agencies in the criminal justice system. Researchers Frank P. Scioli and Thomas J. Cook have assembled 250 books, articles, reports, master's theses, and doctoral dissertations on volunteerism, making their report, published in 1976, the single largest collection of research reports gathered on the subject. In addition to their exhaustive review of the literature, they personally visited, observed, and studied some ongoing volunteer programs. The results of their study showed that the best that could be said about volunteerism was that there is *no evidence that it is less successful* than alternative programs. In fact, they reasoned that it was probably safe to conclude that "volunteer programs performed as well as, or better than, the program alternatives with which they were compared" (Scioli and Cook, 1976).

A noted exception to the rule of quantitatively determined effectiveness has been the volunteer-juvenile offender relationship. As Scioli and Cook (1976: 197) noted, a disproportionate emphasis in the volunteer programs has been placed on juvenile probation/volunteer supervision programs. Perhaps the overemphasis on rehabilitating the juvenile offender and the consequential higher proportion of volunteers used to service the troubled youth account for this evidence of more positive results in this area of volunteerism.

As communities develop programs from the prepared manuals and under the advice and direction of some of the leading authorities, fewer of the errors of the past will be reproduced in the future. Also, instead of volunteer programs being used only in areas where they have demonstrated success, there will be a greater chance for volunteer programs to be utilized in areas of the community that have the greatest need for the programs and/or services. Once an agency has decided to involve citizens, it has to develop a viable, working program through an organizational structure. The establishment of any program involves planning, needs assessment, goal setting, and financial decisions, to achieve the objectives and assessment of those objectives.

SUMMARY

This is the age of active citizen involvement. Citizens participate in public relations groups, in political pressure groups, on citizen review boards or advisory boards, in crime prevention programs, and on operational level interaction groups. Citizens also volunteer their services in myriad other agencies. Although there are pros and cons to the use of volunteers and citizen participation, the con arguments would only limit citizen participation, not eradicate it. Perhaps our society has reached a level of understanding that acknowledges that consumers, even consumers of an administration of justice service, have the right to a voice in decision making (it's their tax dollar, after all). Citizens' opinions are valued, even though an agency might not be legally able to adhere to a citizen's wish.

DISCUSSION QUESTIONS

(1) Are you in favor of civilian review boards? If not, what kind of operation would you put in their place?

(2) Should citizens be able to sue individual officers for their mistakes in the line of duty? Should citizens be able to sue police departments?

(3) Are you in favor of citizen involvement? If not, why? If yes, what restrictions, if any, need to be made?

7

MASS MEDIA RELATIONS

As our American forefathers learned through the Revolutionary War, there is power in the pen and in the press. More recently, Kraus and Davis (1976), in their informative and well-documented book *The Effects of Mass Communication on Political Behavior*, argue that the mass media form a major, if not dominant, institution in the political socialization process in contemporary American society. Their work criticizes traditional studies, which suggest that the mass media (radio, television, newspapers, movies, and so on) play a secondary and supportive role in the process of political socialization. If the mass media can affect attitudes toward certain political candidates, then they can, and often do, affect our perceptions of and expectations for agents in the criminal justice system.

As direct contact with an officer affects citizens' perceptions of the police and their willingness, as victims or as witnesses, to support and report to the police, so does what people hear, read, or see about the police in the mass media. The discussion in this chapter will focus on the two broad purposes of the mass media: (1) the disclosure of information (the right to know) and (2) entertainment, which should give one an understanding of how the fictional role of police can be dominant in the public's mind.

To aid those who are or will someday be working in an agency, the last section of this chapter will also discuss how a police agency can, within its limitations, do its part in establishing better relations with the mass media.

DEFINITION OF MASS MEDIA

"Mass media" means radio, television, movies, newspapers, pamphlets, billboards, and mass demonstrations. The high-speed press, transistor radio, computer linkages, communications satellite, and combinations of these and other technologies have vastly increased the opportunities for worldwide sharing of news and information. "Computers at the Associated Press in New York process 15,000 words a minute. Information moves so fast that only other computers can select and reassign the material" (Sussman, 1979).

THE PURPOSE OF MASS MEDIA

Generally speaking, the mass media serve two broad purposes: (1) the disclosure of information (the right to know) and (2) entertainment.

Disclosure of Information

The disclosure of information is part of the broad concept of freedom of expression, which includes such freedoms as those of speech, the press, and assembly, and the rights of petition and picketing (added in the 1930s). In the 1950s, the Supreme Court added motion pictures, television, and radio. Since that freedom of expression is such an enormously broad concept, the Court, from its beginnings, has been plagued with the problem of determining where to draw the line. Freedom of speech and the press are not absolute rights. They are relative in that they are limited by the coexisting rights of others and the demands of national security and public decency (as in obscenity cases).

What does this have to do with police work? Can offenders, when arrested, call an officer every name except "child of God," and escape punishment for their speech? Yes, unfortunately so. It seems that society expects police officers and correctional personnel to be mature enough to exercise self-control.

To continue this discussion of the disclosure of information and how it affects the criminal justice system, let us look at the so-called freedom of the press. Freedom of the press is part of the freedom of expression. The First Amendment to the Constitution spells it out as follows: "Congress shall make no law abridging the freedom of speech or the press." The mass media collectively become the national "watchdog." Dedicated journalists can and do bring government inefficiency and corruption to the awareness of the general public (as in the Watergate affair).

Too often, however, neither police officers nor journalists fully appreciate the balance between individual civil rights and the public's right to know. Near v. Minnesota (1931) is an important case for our understanding because it was the first major press case to come out of the Supreme Court. It is important for two reasons: (1) its incorporation of the freedom of speech for the states and (2) its use of Blackstone's prior restraint clause. The decision said that because one could not tell whether future editions would be malicious, scandalous, or defamatory, it is better to permit freedom of expression—freedom of the press—and then sue later. In other words, the freedom of the press is so important that in order to flourish, it must do so without censorship. If, however, a newspaper reports materials that are untrue, the newspaper stands to be sued. That is why an efficient newspaper reporter will talk to several persons and get good documentation before publishing any material.

One of the problems within both police agencies and newspaper companies is that they are inundated with information that may not be true. Both the police officer and the journalist have to develop skills to sift through all the materials, to separate the real from the unreal, and to use only those bits of information that are verified. Journalists, therefore, develop contacts for information in much the same way that undercover police do. Journalists, like police, should check and recheck their information before publishing, to avoid being sued and to protect innocent people who can be hurt badly. If and when they do not, they face discipline within their own profession.

Most of the situations experienced by agents in the criminal justice system do not always approach the "interests of many." Fortunately, riots and disturbances are not daily happenings. In the clash between public and individual interests, then, the Court has taken a position of "minimum infringement." That is to say, the government and agents of the criminal justice system as part of that government have to achieve its social goals with the least possible infringement upon First Amendment rights.

An example of how this balancing act might be accomplished comes from the Texas Department of Public Safety, which trains certain police officers as information officers. Their task is to cooperate with reporters, and they also serve as "gatekeepers" for the information needed to complete investigations. Under clear guidelines regarding the news media, access to disaster or emergency scenes, the release of victims' names, and the release of information concerning investigations, the information officer releases accurate and timely facts about the situation in question. The information officer does not cover the story for the media: rather, the officer releases information. This process of coordinating police and news media coverage by trained officers produces a working relationship which honors the limitations and the professionalism of both occupations.

Attitudes of Journalists

Another factor that influences disclosure of information is the attitude of journalists. In a recent survey of police-press relations in

Bloomington, Indiana, journalists showed that they held more liberal views, were more mobile, and felt more socially isolated than did police. Atschull (1975) therefore argued that the hostility between journalists and police may be a function not only of occupation but also of basic temperament.

Remember that journalists are American citizens. If they were socialized to mistrust government, then sometimes they carry those preconceived notions along with them as if they were the cameras to view the world. In addition, motivated by an attitude that an informed public can and does make a difference, journalists view the mass media as performing an extremely important function: to help its audience to understand what is going on so that they can reach an intelligent decision about public affairs. If the publics do not understand crime or the role of the police officer, then the situation will probably never improve. If the people do not understand jails or prisons, the situation of a riot may be viewed as the administrator's fault. With an attitude of societal improvement and fairness, mass media reporting has brought about, either directly or indirectly, improved police management techniques, increased manpower and salaries, better selection and training procedures, removal of corrupt administrators, more efficient court criminal systems and speedier justice, improved criminal procedures, and a host of other benefits to the society at large. Individuals who have sought a more humanistic approach to crime control have valued this role that the mass media can play.

Although many persons have resented the inquisitive nature of journalists who are always rushing to beat a deadline, many persons value the investigative skills which brought to light the Watergate affair and reestablished the need for the public to be informed. In other situations—for example, when specific persons or groups have felt threatened—we often turn to the press to expose corruption. Police officers who take ethical stances often find themselves relying upon the pens of journalists to wage the battle against corruption and abuse in their departments. Because of the attitudes of journalists and the role they play as watchdogs for the society, they take on such a task.

To summarize to this point, one of the purposes of the mass media is to serve as a channel for freedom of expression and the disclosure of information. This worthy goal is limited by the threats of lawsuits and acts of Congress to protect innocent persons and national security. The Constitution also provides for protection against illegal arrest, for protection against illegal invasion of property, for privacy, and for protection against the harm that can be caused by premature news disclosures. Thus, the public does have a right to know—under certain conditions. Journalists worthy of their professional calling verify their information and carefully select materials to be printed in a fashion similar to the way police officers investigate their cases. Since police activities offer a variety of unusual, interesting, and bizarre events, such as murders, major accidents and disasters, and rapes, newspapers assign journalists to work such local areas as police headquarters, the coroner's office, and city hall. The example of the Texas Department of Public Safety, with trained informational officers working within agency guidelines, shows how accurate and timely facts about a situation in question can be released, can produce a working relationship, and can still protect and honor police limitations.

Entertainment

The second primary function of the mass media is entertainment. Police detectives and lawyers have been used as themes by the entertainment media. The point is this: Can the public effectively distinguish between what is news information and what is entertainment? Ethan Katsh and Stephen Arons, both assistant professors in the Legal Studies Program at the University of Massachusetts at Amherst, spent three months watching randomly selected television police programs to answer that question. In particular, they were concerned about the law-abiding image police had on television and what message that role transmitted to viewers.

> They found that almost every episode of almost every police show contained one or more violations of the Fourth, Fifth, or Sixth Amendment guarantees of freedom from unreasonable search and seizure, the right to due process, and the right to counsel. They found further that many viewers failed to detect blatant police-state tactics. They concluded that if police shows are in any sense morality plays, the message communicated is that evil may be subdued by state-sponsored illegality. In short, the end justifies the means [Radelet and Reed, 1975: 420].

The sad point is that many persons cannot distinguish real police work (which they have not seen) from unreal police work (which they see on television all the time). One police officer related this fact when he stopped a truck for speeding. He asked the driver for his driver's license. The male occupant handed his license to the officer with a twenty-dollar bill. The officer exclaimed, "What do you think you are doing?" The sorrowful driver replied, "But that's the way they did it on *Hawaii Five-O!*"

The point is that the media can shape public opinion even in its entertainment. Perhaps no greater illustration of that idea gone awry can be given than through the violence on television.

Unless the logic of the assertion that violence in mass media encourages violent behavior is destroyed by scientifically acceptable evidence, we play dangerous games with the socialization process and its adult products [Wolfgang, 1974: 244].

Similar words could be expressed about the unreal police image portrayed on television. In the past, the mass media not only have directed the attention of the general public along certain lines, but also have played a major role in the formation of public policy (such as that surrounding ecology). The molding of public opinion by the media in terms of police activities may be misleading and may create problems for the police. For example, many television shows have exciting stories, with bad persons as crooks who always get caught by the clever, heroic police officer somewhere between the last commercial and the end of the program. The reality is that many criminal cases are dull. Much police work involves social services (for family disturbances in which there are no good guys or bad guys, for example, or simply for people with problems). The crooks on television tend to be good-looking, well-spoken, and above-average in intelligence. In reality, some of the people caught for their misdoings are caught because they lack intelligence—they are mentally retarded—and some of the real criminals are socially inept individuals with faces that only a mother could love. Moreover (sad yet true), many cases, especially burglaries, remain unsolved.

In short, the mass media need to be made aware of this distortion of police activities and need to prove their responsibility by fairly and accurately reporting the activities of the police—both as an agency and as a group of individual officers. A more realistic image of police on television could help citizens to understand the restraints placed on officers (such as lack of equipment, shortage of personnel, and lack of legal jurisdiction). As long as citizens expect police to be able to arrest persons assaulting each other in their own homes (which police cannot do in more than half of the states), citizens will not look for other solutions to the problem of family disturbances and violence. Rather, they will continue to evaluate the performance of officers based on a standard of behavior that is irrational and illegal in some states.

MASS MEDIA RELATIONS PROGRAMS

Informing communities and enlisting their support for any agency project involves several strategies. The mass media campaign utilizes the popular press to inform and interest the general publics about an agency's endeavors. Some of the resources include newspapers, television, radio, and magazines.

Some basic pros and cons to this method need to be mentioned. First, it attracts the most attention by reaching the broadest possible audience at one specific time. Second, using the mass media for public and community relations can be inexpensive if the paper or television station develops the news. Obviously, it is more expensive if the agency has to pay for the services of a writer to develop the story. Third, if the news medium develops the story, the substance of the message is ultimately decided by writers, editors, and commentators, and the agency usually has little or no control. Thus, the image and basic message to be presented are ultimately determined by the medium, not by the agency or organization. Fourth, stories and reports are not always published or aired. Mass media resources are unpredictable. One of the reasons for this is that competition for print and air space is fierce. Last, an agency's idea of what is newsworthy may not parallel the media's notion of an interesting story. The result is that it requires time and persistence to develop stories and media contacts (Office of Juvenile Justice and Delinquency Prevention, 1978: 5).

Establishing a mass media relations program is just the beginning. A continuing effort will need to be exerted so that working relationships between police and the news media can be maintained. At the heart of the program should be an information officer whose office is an information source. In this matter, then, when there is an emergency or extreme situation, the person to be contacted first by the media will be the information officer. By knowing the types of material needed by crime reporters, the information officer can better anticipate their needs, gather pertinent information in advance, and abate the types of questions that news personnel are bound to ask. Mainly, reporters are looking for a dependable source who can be reliable and provide quick, complete, and accurate information. Reliability, credibility, and trust all take time to establish. Along with the professional behavior comes adherence to voluntary codes of fair practice that have been established by most states dealing with the standards for fair trial and free press. These two rights, as suggested earlier in this chapter, are not meant to be in conflict but, rather, are meant to be complementary. In order for that to happen, both must be accommodated equally and fairly. Thus, most reporters ask only that the information officer fulfill the agency's part of the program. Reporters are seeking out the well-known "five W's and H": Who? What? When? Where? Why? and How? The responsibility of public information officers is to round up this information and pass it on to the news media as quickly and accurately as possible.

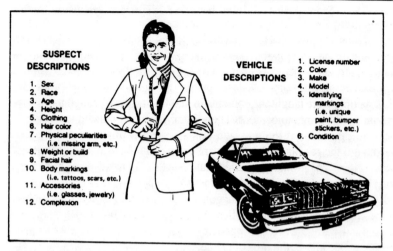

SOURCE: Frinell et al., 1980. Reprinted by permission of the *Journal of Police Science and Administration,* copyright © 1980 by the International Association of Chiefs of Police, Inc., Vol. 8, No. 2, p. 162.

Figure 7.1   Public Announcement in a Newspaper as a Public Education Program

Radio and television reporting is not exactly like newspaper reporting. The broadcast media have different types of programs, depending upon allocated time slots. Moreover, radio and television media like to use taped interviews and other visual experiences to establish credibility and to create the feeling of "on-the-scene" reporting. Therefore, an information officer might have to provide photos for publicity purposes and approved crime-related photos, such as pictures of fugitives; provide for the viewing of weapons used in a crime; and arrange interviews with investigation officers.

The information officer should also develop other news outlets—for example, newswire services and publications in the form of newsletters, brochures, pamphlets, and booklets.

There are many ways to communicate and make sure the publics are informed about the position taken by an agency regarding effective criminal justice activity. The information officer can, thereby, be used to arrange demonstrations of police equipment or tactics for public reviewing via mass media or private showing, by using neighborhood block parties or being an invited speaker for some community organization.

An example of such a public education program comes from an agency in Southern California that desired to increase the accuracy and incidence of citizens' reports of suspicious and criminal activities. The researchers hypothesized that if citizens were instructed as to what details they should note regarding a suspicious person or vehicle, they would be able to give more accurate and complete descriptions. Using the illustration in Figure 7.1, people were taught the contents in that illustration through a newspaper in a public announcement. Then, interviewers contacted various citizens to determine if the message was an effective instructional device. Although the results of this study are based on a limited number of persons (N = 25), it was concluded that once this information was learned, there was a slow rate of memory loss (Frinell et al., 1980).

Other agencies, such as Chicago's Department of Police, have utilized brochures to educate the publics. Some of their information is reproduced in Figure 7.2. Hence, agencies have been using the mass media to teach, especially in the area of crime prevention.

As suggested by the previous example, another strategy to build a better public image or to communicate is to utilize public service announcements. As a requirement of the Federal Communications Commission (FCC), all media are required to set aside airtime or publication space for community projects. These projects usually have to stem from nonprofit, community service activities. The actual announcement may be 10- to 60-second radio or television spots or small advertisements appearing in newspapers or magazines. Since these public service announcements are run at the convenience of the media, there are no guarantees regarding when they will appear. Moreover, because this is "free time" or "free space," there is lots of competition. The organization that wants to utilize this method must provide the necessary copy, advertisements, radio tapes, or videotapes (Office of Juvenile Justice and Delinquency Prevention, 1978: 9).

Even though this particular service is free, an agency or organization may want to consult an art director or commercial artist for professional help in preparing attractive artwork. If the agency is aiming for national markets, then advertisements for national television demand the same level of quality (if not higher) as that of other national commercials. "Also, it is the most expensive kind of public service announcement. (Three television spots, start to finish, may cost between $15,000 and $30,000.)" (Office of Juvenile Justice and Delinquency Prevention, 1978: 10). Because of the large image-building element of this strategy, hiring a professional advertising agency to develop and produce the commercial is advised. If an agency is financially limited, an experienced producer from a local station may assist. Local colleges or schools may

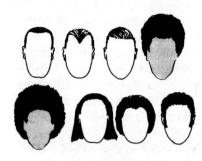

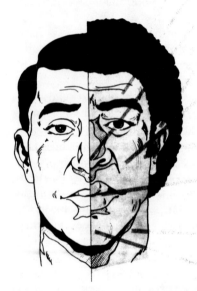

HAIR

Color: Black, brown, red, etc. note if dyed.
Texture: Straight, wavy, curly, tightly curled; note if processed.
Hairline: Low on forehead, receding, "widow's peak" at center, etc.
Style: Neatly combed, unkempt; parted; short, long.

FOREHEAD

Height: High, low, wide, narrow.
Skin: Smooth, light or heavy creases, wrinkled.

NOSE

Shape: Long, wide, flat, pug, Roman, etc.
Nostrils: Wide, narrow, flared.

EARS

Size: Large, small, etc.
Prominence: Protruding or flat against head.

CHEEKS

Flesh: Sunken, filled out, dried, oily.
Wrinkles: "Caliper" lines beside nose, mouth, (if marked); other.

CHEEK BONES

Prominence: High or low, wide or low, also note whether fleshy.

MOUTH

Corners: Turned up, turned down, level.
Upper Lip: Thin, medium, full.
Lower Lip: Thin, medium, full.

NECK

Front: Double chin, protruding Adam's apple, etc.
Sides: Hanging jowls, etc.

CHIN

Shape: Round, oval, pointed, square.
Peculiarities: Small, double, dimpled, cleft.

SOURCE: *How to Describe a Suspect*, June 1975 (revised). Reprinted with permission from the Public and Internal Information Division, Chicago Police Department.

Figure 7.2 How to Describe a Suspect

also volunteer or give free assistance in putting together a special message. Last, but by no means least, an agency can "rent or borrow public service announcements aired or printed by other organizations or the federal/state government, and insert their group's particulars" (Office of Juvenile Justice and Delinquency Prevention, 1978: 11).

Other media possibilities include talk shows, in which an agency spokesperson can discuss a controversy or a trend. Sometimes the editor of a local newspaper or publication will permit an organization a regular column. Letters to the editors may be written in response to other letters sent in to the editorial page. By writing a letter to the editor, an agency can bring public attention to its program or a particular issue surrounding it.

It is important to realize that not all successful mass media relations programs need to be initiated by the police, courts, or correctional departments. Usually, in practice, they do, but the mass media themselves can also initiate programs. The important point is that there can be cooperation (as in the Crime Stoppers program). The use of information officers has been one effective way to create and sustain a mutually beneficial relationship with the press.

SUMMARY

The early American colonists knew the power of the press. That power remains today. While many examples of the mass media's assistance to criminal justice agencies can be documented, the mass media's role has unfortunately been unbecoming, simplified, and stereotyped. In order to break down stereotypes and reduce conflicts, the mass media have been defined and their two general purposes stated: (1) the disclosure of information and (2) entertainment. The disclosure of information is part of the broad concept of freedom of expression which the Supreme Court upholds for citizens as the right to know—under certain conditions. The section on free press and fair trial has showed how these two rights have been brought into a working relationship rather than a conflict. The American Bar Association has been one group pushing for voluntary restrictions by personnel, both in the criminal justice system and in the mass media, so that both the rights of the press and those of trial can be accommodated equally and fairly. The section on mass media relations has given insight into the importance of the information officer and his or her subsequent responsibilities. Much change and professionalization has occurred in the occupations of both the police and the mass media. Both are seemingly more willing to respect each other's professional limitations and to create a working relationship that will meet their needs and accomplish their goals.

DISCUSSION QUESTIONS

(1) Do you agree that the only purposes of the mass media are disclosure of information and entertainment?

(2) Are you in favor of television in the courtroom? What are some of the advantages? disadvantages?

(3) How have the professions of journalism and police work changed to accommodate others?

REFERENCES

ADORNO, T. W., E. FRENKEL-BRUNSWICK, D. J. LEVINSON, and R. N. SANFORD (1950) The Authoritarian Personality. New York: Harper & Row.

ALBRECHT, S. L. and M. GREEN (1977) "Attitudes toward the police and the larger attitude complex: implications for police-community relationships." Criminology 15 (May): 67-86.

ALEX, N. (1969) Black in Blue: A Study of the Negro Policeman. New York: Appleton-Century-Crofts.

ALLPORT, F. H. (1955) Theories of Perception and the Concept of Structure. New York: John Wiley.

ALLPORT, G. W. (1954) The Nature of Prejudice. Reading, MA: Addison-Wesley.

ALTSCHULL, J. H. (1975) "The press and the police: news flow and ideology." Journal of Police Science and Administration 3 (December): 425-433.

American Indian Policy Review Commission (1977) Final Report (Vol. 1). Washington, DC: Government Printing Office.

ATKINS, B. and M. POGREBEN (1976) "Probable causes for police corruption: some theories." Journal of Criminal Justice 4, 1: 9-16.

AUDEN, H. (1981) "Troubled odyssey of Vietnamese fisherman." National Geographic (September).

BANFIELD, D. C. (1970) The Unheavenly City: The Nature and Future of Our Urban Crisis. Boston: Little, Brown.

BARKER, T. (1978) "An empirical study of police deviance other than corruption." Journal of Police Science and Administration 6, 3: 264-272.

——— (1977) "Peer group support for police occupational deviance." Criminology 15, 3: 353-364.

BARNES, H. E. and N. K. TEETERS (1959) New Horizons in Criminology. Englewood Cliffs, NJ: Prentice-Hall.

BEELER, N. F. and F. M. BRANLEY (1951) Experiments in Optical Illusion. New York: Thomas Y. Crowell.

BENT, A. E. and R. A. ROSSUM (1976) Police, Criminal Justice and the Community. New York: Harper & Row.

BERNAYS, E. L. (1952) Public Relations. Norman: University of Oklahoma Press.

BERNSTEIN, D. (1980) "East L.A.'s gang project: prevention or bribery?" Police Magazine 3, 5.

BITTNER, E. (1967) "The police on skid-row: a study of peace keeping." American Sociological Review 32 (October): 699-715.

BLACK, D. J. and A. J. REISS (1967) Patterns of Behavior in Police and Citizen Transactions. Field Survey III, Vol. 2. Washington, DC: President's Commision on Law Enforcement and the Administration of Justice.

BLACKMORE, J. (1979) "CSO's: tedious work but good training." Police Magazine 2, 3: 50-54.

BLAKE, R. R. and J. S. MOUTON (1964) The Managerial Grid. Houston: Gulf.

BORAIKO, A. A. (1981) "The indomitable cockroach." National Geographic 159, 1.

BRODYAGA, L. et al. (1975) Rape and Its Victims: A Report for Citizens, Health Facilities and Criminal Justice Agencies. Washington, DC: National Institute of Law Enforcement and Criminal Justice, Law Enforcement Assistance Administration, and U.S. Department of Labor.

BROPHY, W. A. and S. D. ABERLE (1966) The Indian: America's Unfinished Business. Norman: University of Oklahoma Press.

BROWN v. BOARD OF EDUCATION (1954) 347 U.S. 483

CALIFORNIA PEACE OFFICER (1963) March/April.

CARTER, D. L. (1983) "Hispanic interaction with criminal justice system in Texas: experiences, attitudes, and perceptions." Journal of Criminal Justice 11: 213-227.

CHAVES, F. J. (1976) "Counseling offenders of Spanish heritage." Federal Probation 40 (March).

Chicago Police Department, Public and Internal Information Division (1975) "How to describe a suspect." Chicago Tribune, Sept. 7.

CLEMENTE, F. and M. B. KLEIMAN (1978) "Fear of crime among the aged." Gerontologist 16: 207-210.

COHEN, B. (1980) "Leadership styles of commanders in the New York City Police Department." Journal of Police Science and Administration 8, 2.

COMMONWEALTH v. BROWNMILLER (1900) 14 A.2d 907, 913, 141 Pa. Super; (1940) 14 Atlantic 2d 907.

COREN, S. and J. S. GIRGUS (1978) Seeing Is Deceiving: The Psychology of Visual Illusions. Hillsdale, NJ: Lawrence Erlbaum.

COSTELLO, A. E. (1889) Our Police Protectors. Montclair, NJ: Patterson, Smith.

CRUSE, D. and J. RUBIN (1972) Determinants of Police Behavior. Springfield, VA: National Technical Information.

CULVER, J. (1975) "Policing the police: problems and perspectives." Journal of Police Science and Administration 3, 2: 125-135.

CUTLIP, S. M. and A. H. CENTER (1971) Effective Public Relations (4th ed.). Englewood Cliffs, NJ: Prentice-Hall.

D'ANGELO, S. (1977) "Senior home security program." The Police Chief 44, 2: 60-61.

DANIELS, R. V. (1979) "The 60's: how near was revolution?" Journal of the Institute for Socioeconomic Studies 4 (Winter).

DAUPHINAIS, P. (1979) "Sovereignty and care for the American Indian child: a look to the future." Presented at the annual meeting of the American Psychological Association, New York City.

DAVIS, F. J. (1978) Minority-Dominant Relations: A Sociological Analysis. Arlington Heights, IL: AHM Publishing.

"The Deaf and the Police" (1976) Training Key No. 244.

EHRLICH, H. J. (1973) The Social Psychology of Prejudice. New York: John Wiley.

ERIKSON, K. T. (1966) Wayward Puritans. New York: John Wiley.

ESKELIN, N. (1980) Yes Yes Living in a No No World. Plainfield, NJ: Logos International.

EVERETT, F. L. (1979) "Providing services to American Indian children and families." Presented at the annual meeting of the American Psychological Association, New York City.

Federal Bureau of Investigation (1976) Uniform Crime Reports: 1976 Summary on Law Enforcement Officers Killed. Washington, DC: Government Printing Office.

"Feds bring brutality suit in Philadelphia" (1979) Police Magazine (November): 28-29.

FESTINGER, L. (1964) Conflict, Decision and Dissonance. Stanford, CA: Stanford University Press.

FITZPATRICK, J. P. and L. TRAVIESO PARKER (1981) "Hispanic-Americans in the eastern United States." The Annals of the American Academy of Political and Social Science 454.

FORSLUND, M. A. (1974) "Delinquency among Wind River Indian Reservation youth." Criminology 12, 1: 97-106.

FORWARD, S. and C. BUCK (1978) Betrayal of Innocence: Incest and Its Devastation. Los Angeles: J. P. Tarcher.

FOSDICK, R. B. (1920) American Police Systems. Montclair, NJ: Patterson, Smith.

FOX, H. G., M. J. LATZEN, and F. H. VASQUEZ (1978) "Senior citizens." Law and Order 26.

FRENCH, L. A. (1980) "Anomie and violence among Native Americans." International Journal of Comparative and Applied Criminal Justice 4, 1.

FRINELL, D. E., E. DAHLSTROM III, and D. A. JOHNSON (1980) "A public education program designed to increase the accuracy and incidence of citizens' reports of suspicious and criminal activities." Journal of Police Science and Administration 8, 2: 160-165.

GRENCIK, J. and H. M. SNIBBE (1973) Physiological Fitness Standards for Police. Los Angeles: Los Angeles County Sheriff's Department.

GRIGGS v. DUKE POWER COMPANY (1971) 915 S. Ct. 847

HAGEMAN, M. J. C. (1978) "Occupation of stress and marital relationships." Journal of Police Science and Administration 6: 402-412.

HAKKEN, J. (1979) Discrimination Against Chicanos in the Dallas Rental Housing Market: An Experimental Extension of the Housing Market Practices Survey. Washington, DC: U.S. Department of Housing and Urban Development, Office of Policy Development and Research.

HALL, J., M. WILLIAMS and L. TOMAINO (1966) "The challenge of commitment." Journal of Criminal Law, Criminology and Police Science 57, 4: 493-503.

HAREL, Z. and K. BRODERICK (1980) "Victimization and fear of crime among the urban aged." The Police Chief 47 (March).

HARRIES, K. D. (1974) The Geography of Crime and Justice. New York: McGraw-Hill.

HARRINGTON, M. (1969) The Other America: Poverty in the United States. New York: Macmillan.

HART, W. (1980) "The power of sheriff pitches." Police Magazine 3, 6: 49-55.

HAVINGHURST, R. J. (1978) "Indian education since 1960." The Annals of the American Academy of Political and Social Science 451.

Hill and Knowlton Executives (1975) Critical Issues in Public Relations. Englewood Cliffs, NJ: Prentice-Hall.

HILTS, S. L. (1971) Crime, Power and Morality. Scranton, PA: Chandler.

HOREJSI, C. R. (1973) "Training for the direct-service volunteer in probation." Federal Probation 37, 3: 38-41.

"Houston: claims of reform" (1979) Police Magazine (November): 29.

HRABA, J. (1979) American Ethnicity. Itasca, IL: F. E. Peacock.

"The Indian and the frontier in American history: a need for revision" (1973) Western Historical Quarterly (January).

INSTITUTE FOR SOCIOECONOMIC STUDIES (1981) Socioeconomic Newsletter 6, 2.

JAYCOX, V. H. (1978) "The elderly's fear of crime: rational or irrational?" Victimology 3: 329-334.

JORDAN, V. E. (1980) "Black-white inequality is getting worse." Wichita Eagle and Beacon (May 11): 3B.

KALVEN, H. and H. ZEISEL (1971) The American Jury. Chicago: University of Chicago Press.

KIERNAN, M. (1979) "Police vs. the press: 'there's always tension.' " Police (July): 38-43.

KLYMAN, F. T. (1974) "The police-community relations survey: a qualitative inventory of services and work units." Journal of Police Science and Administration 2, 1: 77-81.

———and J. KRUCKENBERG (1979) "A national survey of police community relations unit." Journal of Police Science and Administration 7 (March): 72-79.

KNUDSON, D. C. (1979) Environmental Health Facilities Evaluation for the Papago Tribe of Arizona. AZ: Stram Engineers.

KRAJICK, K. (1980) "Police vs. police." Police Magazine 3, 3: 6-14.

KRAUS, S. and D. DAVIS (1976) The Effects of Mass Communication on Political Behavior. University Park: Pennsylvania State University Press.

LANE, R. (1889) Policing the City, Boston: 1822-1885. Montclair, NJ: Patterson, Smith.

The Life and Teachings of Jesus and His Apostles (2nd ed.) (1979) Salt Lake City: Church of Jesus Christ of the Latter-Day Saints.

LOCKARD, J. L., J. T. SKIP DUNCAN, and R. N. BRENNER (1978) Director of Community Crime Prevention. Washington, DC: Law Enforcement Assistance Administration and National Institute of Law Enforcement and Criminal Justice.

MATHIS, A. (1978) "Contrasting approaches to the study of black families." Journal of Marriage and the Family (November).

MATTHEWS, C. V., P. ROMPLER, R. VANDEER, and G. KIEFER (1969) Participation of Volunteers in Correctional Programs: An International Perspective. IL: Center for the Study of Crime, Delinquency and Corrections.

McADOO, H. P. (1978) "Factors related to stability in upward mobile black families." Journal of Marriage and the Family (November).

McDOWELL, C. P. (1975) Police in the Community. Cincinnati: W. H. Anderson.

McLEMORE, S. D. (1980) Racial and Ethnic Relations in America. Boston: Allyn & Bacon.

McLENNAN, K. and M. LOVELL, Jr. (1981) "Immigration reform: an economic necessity." Journal of the Institute for Socioeconomic Studies 6, 2.

MILLER, D. (1980) "The deaf community is calling." The Police Chief 47 (April).

MITZGER, P. L. (1971) "American sociology and black assimilation: conflicting perspectives." American Journal of Sociology 76 (January).

MUNN, N. L. (1961) Psychology: The Fundamentals of Human Adjustment (4th ed.). Boston: Houghton Mifflin.

MYRDAL, G. (1944) An American Dilemma. New York: Harper & Brothers.

National Advisory Commission on Civil Disorders (1968) Report. Washington, DC: Government Printing Office.

National Advisory Commission on Criminal Justice Standards and Goals (1976) "Corrections and the community: national standards and goals," in R. M. Carter and L. T. Wilkens (eds.) Probation, Parole and Community Corrections (2nd ed.). New York: John Wiley.

———(1973) A National Strategy to Reduce Crime. Washington, DC: Government Printing Office.

NEAR v. MINNESOTA, 283 U.S. 697; 51 S. Ct. 625; 75 L. Ed. 1357

NIEDERHOFFER, A. (1967) Behind the Shield: The Police in Urban Society. Garden City, NY: Doubleday.

NOBLES, W. E. (1978) "Toward an empirical and theoretical framework for defining black families." Journal of Marriage and the Family (November).

NOVA INSTITUTE (1978) Crime Against the Elderly: The Role of the Criminal Justice System in New York City. New York: Author.

Office of Juvenile Justice and Delinquency Prevention (1978) Publicity Strategies. Washington, DC: Law Enforcement Assistance Administration.

PACHON, H. P. and J. W. MOORE (1981) "Mexican Americans." The Annals of the American Academy of Political and Social Science 454.

PEEBLES, P. (1980) "Dealing with persons having handicapping conditions." The Police Chief 47 (March).

PETTIBONE, J. M. (1973) "Community-based programs: catching up with yesterday and planning for tomorrow." Federal Probation 37 (September).

PILIAVIN, I. and S. BRIAR (1964) "Police encounters with juveniles." American Journal of Sociology 70 (September): 206-214.

PLESSY v. FERGUSON (1896) 163 U.S. 537; 16 S. Ct. 1138; 41 L. Ed. 256

POUND, R. (1960) "Discretion dispensation and mitigation: the problem of the individual special case." New York University Review 35: 925-926.

President's Commission on Law Enforcement and the Administration of Justice (1967) The Challenge of Crime in a Free Society. Washington, DC: Government Printing Office.

RADELET, L. A. and REED (1975) The Police and the Community. New York: Macmillan.

RAPAPORT, A. (1950) Science and the Goals of Man: A Study in Semantic Orientation. New York: Harper & Row.

REIMERS, D. M (1981) "Post-World War II immigration to the United States: America's latest newcomers." The Annals of the American Academy of Political and Social Science 454.

Report on Federal, State and Tribal Jurisdiction (1976) Final Report to the American Indian Policy Review Commission. Washington, DC: Government Printing Office.

RICHARDSON, J. F. (1970) The New York Police: Colonial Times to 1901. New York: Oxford University Press.

ROBIN, G. D. (1980) Introduction to the Criminal Justice System. New York: Harper & Row.

ROBINSON, J. O. (1972) The Psychology of Visual Illusion. London: Hutchinson.

ROGERS, C. R. (1951) Client-Centered Therapy. Boston: Houghton Mifflin.

ROSE, P. I. (1964) They and We. New York: Random House.

RUSSELL, H. E. and A. BEIGEL (1976) Understanding Human Behavior for Effective Police Work. New York: Basic Books.

SAENGER, G. H. (1953) The Social Psychology of Prejudice. New York: Harper & Brothers.

SCHEIER, I. H. et al. (1972) Guides and Standards for the Use of Volunteers in Correctional Programs. Washington, DC: Law Enforcement Assistance Administration.

SCHULZ, D. A. (1970) "The role of the boyfriend in lower-class Negro life," in C. V. Willie (ed.) The Family Life of Black People. Columbus, OH: Charles E. Merrill.

SCIOLI, F. P., Jr. and T. J. COOK (1976) "How effective are volunteers? Public participation in the criminal justice system." Crime and Delinquency (April): 192-200.

SENN, M. (1952) A Study of Police Training Programs in Minority Relations. Los Angeles: Law Enforcement Committee of the Los Angeles County Conference on Community Relations.

SHEARER, W. T., J. H. DELLINGER, W. A. McCARTY, and A. E. WAISGERBER (1977) "The law enforcement explorer: an integral part of the police team." The Police Chief 44, 7.

SHILLER, S. A. (1972) "More light on a law visibility function: the need to recognize and structure selective discriminatory enforcement of laws." Police Law Quarterly (Summer): 15.

SHRIVER, S. (1965) "How goes the war on poverty?" Look (July 27).

SIMPSON, G. E. and M. YINGER, Jr. (1972) Racial and Cultural Minorities: An Analysis of Prejudice and Discrimination (4th ed.). New York: Harper & Row.

SLAUGHTER, E. L. (1976) Indian Child Welfare: A Review of the Literature. Denver: Center for Social Research and Development, Denver Research Institute, University of Denver.

SKOLNICK, J. H. (1977) Justice Without Trial: Law Enforcement in a Democratic Society. New York: John Wiley.

SMITH, P. E. and R. O. HAWKINS (1973) "Victimization, types of citizen-police contacts, and attitudes toward the police." Law and Society (Fall): 135-152.

SOURYAL, S. S. (1977) Police Administration and Management. St. Paul, MN: West Publishing Company.

SPEIR, W. E. (1977) "News media relations: a key ingredient in developing community involvements." The Police Chief 44, 4: 18-19.

STANLEY, S. and R. K. THOMAS (1978) "Current social and demographic trends among North American Indians." The Annals of the American Academy of Political and Social Science 436.

STARK, R. (1972) Police Riots, Collective Violence and Law Enforcement. Belmont, CA: Wadsworth.

STATE v. TINDELL (1922) 112 Kan. 256, 210.

STEINER, S. (1968) The New Indians. New York: Harper & Row.

SUE, S., D. B. ALLEN, and L. CONAWAY (1978) "The responsiveness and equality of mental health care to Chicanos and Native Americans." American Journal of Community Psychology 6: 137-146.

SUSSMAN, L. R. (1979) "Mass media: opportunities and threats." The Annals of the American Academy of Political and Social Science 442.

SWAN, L. A. (1977) "The politics of identification: a perspective of police accountability," in P. F. Cromwell, Jr., and G. Keefer (eds.) Police-Community Relations (2nd ed.). St. Paul, MN: West Publishing Company.

TAFT, P. B., Jr. (1979) "Religious reformers want to proclaim liberty to the captives." Corrections Magazine 5, 4: 36-43.

TATUM, W. M. (1978) "The importance of Spanish language training for law enforcement officers." The Police Chief 45, 3.

TEEUBER, C. M. (1976) Case Study: The Location of a Playground. Washington, DC: U.S. Bureau of the Census.

TENNESSEE v. GARNER (1985) 105 S. Ct. 1694.

TERRITO, L., C. R. SWANSON, Jr., and N. C. CHAMELIN (1977) The Police Personnel Selection Process. Indianapolis, IN: Bobbs-Merrill.

THORPE v. RUTLAND AND BURLINGTON RAILROAD COMPANY (1874) 27 Vt. 140.

TICE v. STATE INDUS. ACC. COMMISSION, STATE OF OREGON (1900) 195 P.2d 188, 191, 183 Or. 593.

TIDYMAN, E. (1974) Dummy. Boston: Little, Brown.

TOMAINO, L. (1975) "The five faces of probation." Federal Probation 49, 4: 42-45.

TROJANOWICZ, R. C. (1972) "Police-community relations: problems and process." Criminology (February): 401-424.

UNGER, S. (1977) The Destruction of American Indian Families. New York: Association of American Indian Affairs.

United Nations (1976) "The origin of probation in the United States," in R. M. Carter and L. T. Wilkens (eds.) Probation, Parole and Community Corrections (2nd ed.). New York: John Wiley.

UNITED STATES v. CHICAGO, M, ST. PAUL AND P. R. COMPANY (1931) 282 U.S. 311 at 324, 51 S.Ct. 159, 75l. Ed. 359.

THE URBAN POLICE FUNCTION / WIS. STATS. 62.09 (13) Sec. p. 117.

U.S. EX REL ACCARDI v. SHAUGNESSY (1953) N.Y., 71 St. Ct. 499, 503, 347, U.S. 360, 98 L.Ed.

U.S. House Select Committee on Aging (1981) Elder Abuse: An Examination of a Hidden Problem. Washington, DC: Government Printing Office.

VERNON, G. M. (1965) Human Interaction. New York: Ronald Press.

WAGNER, A. E. (1980) "Citizen complaints against the police: the complainant." Journal of Police Science and Administration 8, 3: 247-252.

WARNER, W. L. and P. S. LUNT (1941) The Status System of a Modern Community. New Haven, CT: Yale University Press.

WASHINGTON v. DAVIS (1976) 96 S.Ct. 2040

WEISMAN, A. D. (1979) "Coping with untimely death," in Stanley Nass (ed.) Crisis Intervention. Dubuque, IA: Kendall/Hunt.

WHITEHOUSE, J. E. (1973) "Historical perspectives on the police community service function." Journal of Police Science and Administration 2: 87-92.

WILLIS, R. L. (1976) "Senior citizen crime prevention program." The Police Chief 43, 2.

WILSON, J. Q. (1968) Varieties of Police Behavior. Cambridge, MA: Harvard University Press.

WILSON, O. W. and R. C. McLAREN (1977) Police Administration (4th ed.). New York: McGraw-Hill.

WIRTH, L. (1928) The Ghetto. Chicago: University of Chicago Press.

WOLFGANG, M. E. (1974) "Violent behavior," in A. S. Blumberg (ed.) Current Perspectives on Criminal Behavior. New York: Alfred A. Knopf.

YAKES, N. and D. AKEY [eds.] (1980) Encyclopedia of Associations. Detroit: Gale Research.

YIN, R. L., M. E. VOGEL, J. M. CHAIKEN, and D. R. BOTH (1976) Patrolling the Neighborhood Beat: Residents and Residential Security, Executive Summary. Santa Monica, CA: Rand Corporation.

YOUNG RIFAI, M. A. (1976) Older Americans' Crime Prevention Research Project: Final Report. Portland, OR: Multnomah County Public Safety Division.

INDEX

ABOUT THE AUTHOR

MARY J. HAGEMAN, Ph.D., is an accomplished and disciplined writer, speaker, and trainer. Some of her publications include *Community Corrections* (which she coauthored) and articles in such leading journals as the *Journal of Police Science and Administration*. She has served on the faculty of six major colleges and universities, most recently with Virginia Commonwealth University in Richmond. She is Director of Omega Foundation, which provides workshops and seminars to public and private agencies to help assess departmental climates and to help employees increase efficiency, teamwork, and productivity by learning to understand our multicultural, multiracial society.